TEXT AND PHOTOGRAPHY: **MARTIN NORDIN**
DESIGN AND ILLUSTRATIONS: **LI SÖDERBERG** AND **KATY KIMBELL**

GREEN
BURGERS

Creative vegetarian recipes
for burgers and sides

MARTIN NORDIN

hardie grant books

[contents]

why a book on green burgers?

When I first started thinking about this book, I was struck by how liberating and creative it is to devise, prepare and eat green burgers. Whereas a classic meat-based burger is indeed uncompromisingly classic - this is what it looks like, this is how to prepare it, it has to be grilled ... no, actually fried... and then there are these accompaniments and nothing else, that's it - what goes into a green burger is far less restricted. There's not *one* classic - you have free rein! Do what you want, experiment, go for it, question what a burger can be. See it as a sociable way of eating, informal and simple, and create things you like. I want to inspire you to have the courage to try out different variants, so you can then start to create your own favourite, try it out again, mix the accompaniments, discover something else and create a completely new favourite.

For me, it's an ongoing process of cutting down on meat and eating fewer animal products overall. If you care about the environment, reducing your meat consumption is a no-brainer. But what's more, in recent years, I've also learnt to appreciate vegetables in a completely new way. My focus has shifted away from ingrained patterns and preconceptions about what a meal should be like; I now take my own thoughts about flavour, consistency and composition as my starting point and ponder on them. (Personally I'd welcome the death of the meat-centred model for a plate of food, once and for all.)

When I cook, the context is at least as important as the food. I like the whole idea of gathering around a meal and getting the opportunity to spend time with friends and family who are into eating and cooking and who like grazing, raw materials, tips and tricks. The best meals are the ones where everyone is part of the process; ideally there will be lots of accompaniments that are either prepared on site or that the guests bring with them as contributions, alternated with things that have been maturing for weeks. You can then create something together, with everyone adapting their plate to whatever excites them. Are you mad about that caramelised onion? Yes, so take an extra dollop and to hell with the pickled gherkins that I always used to remove when I ate burgers as a child. Or try them out and re-evaluate them! Be daring and try some pickled radish - even if it smells a bit funky it tastes so great.

MARTIN NORDIN

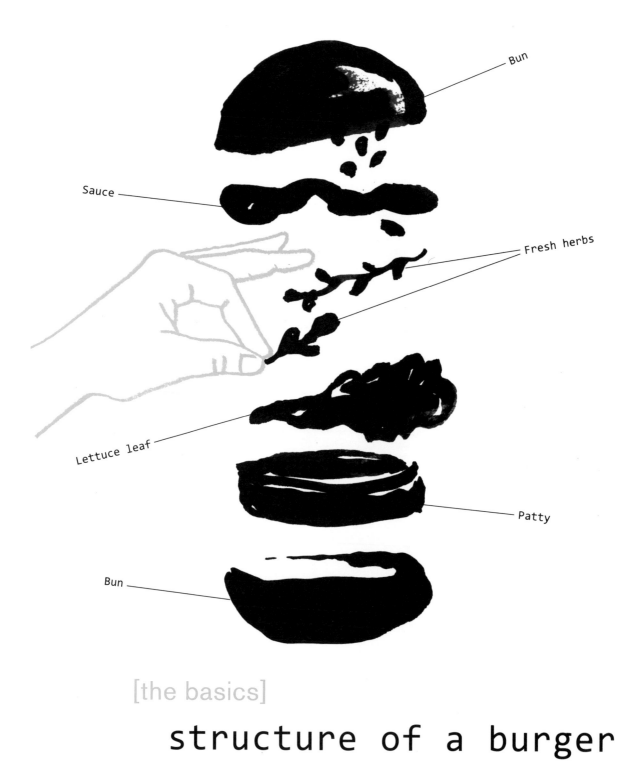

Bun

Sauce

Fresh herbs

Lettuce leaf

Patty

Bun

[the basics]

structure of a burger

Many of the recipes in this book are inspired by dishes that I've eaten and that have seemed ideal for deconstructing and reconstructing between two slices of bread. Just as with all cooking, the art lies in creating a wicked burger largely at the interface between different textures and flavours. It's all about balance. If the patty is deep-fried and crispy maybe you'll need something acidic to counterbalance the greasy taste. If part of the burger seems on the dry side – for example, if the patty is based on legumes – maybe some mayonnaise would even things out.

The patty: Most patties improve if they're left to rest in the fridge for a few hours before you cook them. It's a good idea to prepare bean patties the evening before, and then cook them for supper the day after. Patties for deep-frying are best if you freeze them first.

Lettuce leaves and other greens: Forget everything you've heard about lettuce always having to be at the bottom of the burger - totally immaterial if you ask me. For my part, I think there's often a bit too much of an emphasis on lettuce - there are, after all, quite a lot of other greens in these burgers.

The bun: I've used several different buns for burgers, and you'll find my favourite ones on pages 94-103. The choice of bun should be based on the flavour of the patty. A slightly sweeter brioche bun goes excellently with a salty bean patty, whilst a patty made of Jerusalem artichokes – which are slightly sweet – would maybe go better with a crispy bun based on poolish (a kind of starter). Or just leave out the bun entirely and serve the patty in a lettuce leaf instead.

The sauce: If the recipe includes mayonnaise, ketchup, a herb sauce or a creamy miso sauce, this is to contribute juiciness or counterbalance acidity. I usually serve the sauce on the side, so everyone can add it according to their own taste.

Fresh herbs: Do sprinkle on plenty of fresh herbs - maybe even instead of lettuce leaves. Is the herb in flower? Make use of that! Most herb flowers are edible and create a further dimension - both flavour-wise and visually.

making the job easier

You can easily go over the top with special utensils, but there are good ones that I simply find it hard to do without when I'm cooking.

Knife: A good (and nice-looking!) knife. Keep it sharp and, whatever you do, *always* wash it by hand!

Food ring: A food ring is unbeatable for shaping perfect bean patties, and it also helps hold together patties that would otherwise easily spread over the frying pan (skillet). Buy food rings in different sizes so you can adjust the patty size to the bun size.

Grater: Invest in a really good grater for small jobs such as grating lemon zest, cheese or truffles. I ve tried out several makes, but nothing beats the Microplane.

Digital scales: Sometimes, such as when baking, you simply need more precise weights, and that's where digital scales come in.

Digital thermometer: There's a huge range on the market, but many of them are absolutely useless. Loads of them have packed in on me, so invest in a really good one. Essential for deep-frying, but also good for checking that the patties are cooked through.

Wooden spoon: For scraping up stuff that otherwise easily sticks to the bottom of the saucepan, a wooden spoon is unbeatable.

Salad spinner: Good for removing liquid from beans or getting lettuce crispy after an ice bath.

Slotted spoon: Essential for deep-frying – for pushing round, turning and lifting things out.

Flat griddle pan: Cooking bean patties on a grill can be tricky – they easily get stuck, and after a while half the burger will have fallen through the bars. Buy a flat griddle pan and brush the patties generously with some oil – problem solved!

Spatula: Handy when you want to get that little bit more out of the bowl.

Mandoline: To get really thin slices and julienne strips. For me, it's nearly as important as a good knife.

Kitchen tweezers: For twirling up potato strips, lifting a sage leaf out of the fryer or just removing something. You never know when you'll need them, so have them close at hand.

Washing-up brush: Having things clean and ship-shape on the draining board and washing up as you go whilst cooking are at least as important as having all the ingredients in place when you start off.

burgers

Question what a burger is, and off you go
with legumes, root vegetables, mushrooms,
cheese or whatever you happen to feel like.
My exploration into the area led to these
31 favourites.

#01

BORLOTTI AND CHANTERELLE
BURGER WITH LINGONBERRY CHUTNEY

- -

For 6 burgers:

300 g (10½ oz) Oven-Baked Onions (see page 132)
150 g (5 oz/2½ cups) cooked borlotti beans
300 g (10½ oz) chanterelles
rapeseed oil for frying
1 tbsp butter
3 tbsp Almond Butter or other Nut Butter (see page 149)
100 g (3½ oz/scant ½ cup) boiled red rice
pinch of sea salt

Lingonberry chutney:

4 medium shallots
4 tbsp butter
4 tbsp cane sugar
240 g (8½ oz) lingonberries or cranberries
2 tbsp white wine vinegar
2 tbsp finely chopped chilli
2 tsp grated fresh ginger
bay leaf

To serve:
6 burger buns
butter for the buns
300 g (10½ oz) Västerbotten or other strong
*   hard cheese, cut into sticks*
fresh parsley

Instructions:

1. Bake the onions for the patties according to the recipe on page 132.

2. Rinse the beans in cold water and drain in a colander.

3. Trim and clean the chanterelles and cut into small pieces. Heat a little oil in a frying pan (skillet) until it starts to smoke. Toss in the chanterelles and flash-fry them until they have developed some colour and start to shrink. Reduce the heat, add the butter and stir until it has melted. Remove the frying pan from the heat and allow to cool.

4. Put the oven-baked onions, the almond butter and rice into a food processor and mix so that the ingredients are blended properly. Pour in the borlotti beans and pulse-blend or mix quickly for a few seconds – the beans must just be broken up a little. Throw in the chanterelles and turn them with a spoon so that everything is well combined (don't overmix!). Add a little salt to taste.

5. Take a handful of mixture at a time and shape into 6 round patties, either by hand or using a food ring (see page 10). Place the patties on a large plate and cover with cling film (plastic wrap). Leave in the fridge for at least an hour, preferably longer, so they will hold together better when you fry them.

6. Preheat the oven to 180°C (350°F/Gas 4).

7. To make the chutney, peel and halve the shallots lengthways. Put them into a cold saucepan, add the butter and put the saucepan over a medium heat. Put the lid on and simmer for about 15 minutes. Stir with a wooden spoon now and then so they don't burn, then increase the heat, add the sugar and brown for about 30 seconds so the sugar dissolves. Reduce the heat, then add the remainder of the ingredients. Simmer gently for 30 minutes without a lid until the consistency is creamy – almost sticky. Stir with a wooden spoon every so often.

8. Meanwhile heat a few tablespoons of oil in a frying pan over a medium heat. Fry the patties for a few minutes on both sides until they have developed a nice colour. Transfer the patties to an ovenproof dish and bake them in the oven for 5–10 minutes.

9. Butter the buns on the cut surface and fry them quickly in a frying pan or grill (broil) them in the oven.

10. Place a patty on the bottom of each bun. Top with cheese sticks, spoon over some lingonberry chutney and scatter with sprigs of parsley.

- -

#02

DEEP-FRIED MUSHROOM AND QUINOA BURGER WITH PURPLE SAUERKRAUT AND GARLIC MAYONNAISE

- -

For 6 burgers:

4 medium shallots
2 tbsp rapeseed oil
2 tbsp dark malt or red wine vinegar
2 tbsp butter
400 g (14 oz) field mushrooms, ideally chestnut mushrooms
2–3 tbsp Dry-Roasted Walnuts (see page 149)
400 g (14 oz/2 cups) boiled quinoa
1 tbsp deseeded finely chopped chilli
140 g (5 oz/1½ cups) grated Parmesan
25 g (1 oz/scant ½ cup) panko breadcrumbs
2 eggs

Breading and deep-frying:
120 g (4 oz/generous ¾ cup) plain (all-purpose) flour
3 eggs
75 g (2½ oz/1¼ cups) panko breadcrumbs
75 g (2½ oz/scant ½ cup) boiled quinoa
1 litre (34 fl oz/4 cups) peanut oil
salt

To serve:
6 burger buns
butter for the buns
Purple Sweetheart Cabbage and
  Apple Sauerkraut (see page 120)
Pickled Mustard Seeds (see page 136)
Garlic Mayonnaise (see page 128)

Instructions:

1. To make the patties, peel and finely chop the shallots. Heat up 1 tablespoon of the rapeseed oil in a frying pan (skillet) and brown the shallots until they start to develop some colour. Pour in the vinegar and reduce to a sticky mixture. Reduce the heat and add 1 tablespoon of the butter. Stir until the butter has melted and the onions are glazed. Transfer to a bowl and allow to cool.

2. Clean and finely chop the mushrooms. Dry out the frying pan in which you fried the onions, pour in the remaining rapeseed oil and heat until the oil starts to smoke. Toss in the mushrooms and flash-fry them until they start to develop colour and shrink. Reduce the heat and add the remaining butter. Stir until the butter has melted. Transfer the mushrooms to the bowl of onions.

3. Toast the walnuts as described on page 149. Crush about 2–3 tablespoons of the walnuts in a mortar and turn them into the bowl (you can store the remainder in a well-sealed jar). Add the quinoa, chilli, Parmesan, panko breadcrumbs and eggs. Stir until everything is well combined.

4. Take a handful of mixture at a time and shape into 6 round patties, either by hand or using a food ring (see page 10). Put the patties on a large plate and cover with cling film (plastic wrap). Put in the freezer for a few hours, until firm. This will make the breading and deep-frying easier.

5. Preheat the oven to 180°C (350°F/Gas 4).

6. Pour the flour into a bowl. Crack the eggs into another bowl and lightly whisk them. Mix the panko breadcrumbs and quinoa in a third bowl. Take the patties out of the freezer and turn them first in the flour, then in the whisked egg and finally in the panko mixture.

7. Pour the peanut oil into a high-sided saucepan over a high heat until it reaches 190°C (375°F), then reduce the heat to medium and try to keep the oil at 190°C (375°F). Deep-fry the patties 2 at a time for 2–3 minutes, until they are golden brown. Push them around with a slotted spoon now and again.

8. Lift the patties out and lay them on a paper towel-lined plate so any excess oil can run off. Salt them on both sides.

9. Transfer the patties to an ovenproof dish and bake them in the oven for 5–10 minutes.

10. Butter the buns on the cut surface and fry them quickly in a frying pan or grill (broil) them in the oven.

11. Put a little sauerkraut on the bottom of each bun. Put a patty on top, spoon over some pickled mustard seeds and add a dash of mayonnaise.

- -

#03

COURGETTE BURGER WITH GRILLED SPRING ONIONS AND WILD GARLIC

- -

For 6 burgers:

100 g (3½ oz/generous ⅓ cup) butter
120 g (4 oz/generous ¾ cup) plain (all-purpose) flour
1 tsp baking powder
pinch of sea salt
100 ml (3½ fl oz/scant ½ cup) milk
1 egg
100 ml (3½ fl oz/scant ½ cup) cold water
25 g (1 oz/scant ½ cup) panko breadcrumbs
2 medium courgettes (zucchini)
butter for frying

Grilled spring onions (scallions):
2 tsp Roasted Pepper Seasoning (see page 132)
2–3 tbsp rapeseed oil
1 tsp sesame oil
sea salt
6 spring onions (scallions)

To serve:
1 bunch of wild garlic or chives
6 burger buns
butter for the buns
a little Sriracha sauce or Kimchi as necessary
  (see pages 140–143)

Instructions:

1. Preheat the oven to 180°C (350°F/Gas 4).

2. Melt the butter over a low heat.

3. Mix the flour, baking powder and salt in a bowl. Add the milk and egg and whisk together to form an even, fairly thick batter. Stir in the butter and water, then fold in the panko breadcrumbs. Put to one side.

4. Finely shred the courgettes with a mandoline, preferably using a grating attachment. You can also coarsely grate the courgettes with a normal grater, but bear in mind that the courgettes will then release liquid, which you must remove.

5. Put the courgette strips on a baking tray and douse them with the batter (see photo on previous page).

6. Heat a frying pan (skillet) and put in a knob of butter. Transfer a little of the courgette mixture at a time to the frying pan using a fork, and form small courgette pancakes. Fry for a minute or so on both sides so they take on a golden colour. If you want you can use a food ring (see page 10) to start with, so the courgette pancakes hold together better, in which case you should put the food ring straight into the frying pan and fill it with the courgette mixture.

7. Transfer the courgette pancakes to an ovenproof dish and bake in the oven for 5–10 minutes.

8. Make the roasted pepper seasoning as described on page 132. Put 2 teaspoons of the pepper seasoning into a large plastic bag. Pour in the rapeseed oil, sesame oil and salt. Put to one side. You can of course add other seasoning such as garlic and chilli if you wish, for extra flavour and heat.

9. Cook the spring onions on a barbecue or fry them in a dry frying pan over a high heat, allowing them to develop a little colour. Put the onions into the bag of marinade, tie the top and leave for 10–15 minutes so the spring onions steam in their own heat (see pages 148–149).

10. Chop the wild garlic or chives. If you can get hold of wild garlic with flowers or buds then use them too. They not only look nice but also have a lovely mild flavour reminiscent of roasted garlic.

11. Butter the buns on the cut surface and fry them quickly in a frying pan or grill (broil) them in the oven.

12. Put two courgette pancakes on each bun and top with spring onions and wild garlic, and a little Sriracha sauce or kimchi as necessary.

#04

BLACK BEAN BURGER WITH CHEDDAR AND CARAMELISED ONIONS

For 6 burgers:

400 g (14 oz/2½ cups) cooked black beans
rapeseed or peanut oil for frying
65 g (2¼ oz/scant ½ cup) finely chopped onion
1 tsp mild chilli powder, e.g. piment d'Espelette
1 tsp smoked paprika powder
3 tbsp BBQ sauce
50 g (2 oz/scant ½ cup) Dry-Roasted Walnuts (see page 149)
2 tbsp finely chopped fresh coriander (cilantro)
100 g (3½ oz/scant ½ cup) boiled black rice
25 g (1 oz/scant ½ cup) panko breadcrumbs
sea salt

Caramelised onions:

2 onions
2 tbsp butter
1 tbsp red wine vinegar

To serve:

120 g (4 oz) Cheddar
6 burger buns
butter for the buns
cos lettuce

Instructions:

1. Rinse the beans in cold water and drain in a colander.
2. Heat a little oil in a frying pan (skillet) and fry the onions over a fairly high heat until they have taken on colour and are on the verge of burning.
3. Reduce the heat, add the chilli and paprika powders and stir. Stir in the BBQ sauce and take the frying pan off the heat.
4. Roast the walnuts as described on page 149.
5. Chop the walnuts and put them in a bowl together with the beans, coriander, rice, panko breadcrumbs and a pinch of salt. Mix the ingredients together with a potato masher (the beans should only be lightly mashed). Add the onion mixture and stir so that everything is well combined.

6. Take a handful of mixture at a time and shape into 6 round patties, either by hand or using a food ring (see page 10). Put the patties on a large plate and cover with cling film (plastic wrap). Put in the fridge for at least an hour, preferably longer, so that they will hold together better when you fry them.
7. For the caramelised onions, peel and chop the onions and put them into a cold saucepan. Add the butter and put the saucepan over a medium heat, and then put the lid on. The onions will soon start to release liquid, and the flavours will be concentrated as a result of their cooking in their own juices. Stir with a wooden spoon about once every 5 minutes for 30–40 minutes, and check they are not burning. (If you notice they're starting to get dry you can add the vinegar earlier.)
8. Remove the lid, pour over the vinegar, raise the heat and cook for about 15 minutes, stirring, until considerably reduced. Set aside.
9. Preheat the oven to 180°C (350°F/Gas 4).
10. Heat a few tablespoons of the oil in a frying pan over a medium heat. Fry the patties for a few minutes on both sides until they have developed a nice colour. Transfer them to an ovenproof dish. Put a few slices of cheese on each patty, place in the oven and leave until the cheese has melted.
11. Butter the buns on the cut surface and fry them quickly in a frying pan or grill (broil) them in the oven.
12. Place a patty on the bottom of each bun. Put a cos lettuce leaf on top and slap on a generous spoonful of the caramelised onion.

#05

BLACK BEAN BURGER WITH BABA GHANOUSH, GRILLED SPRING ONIONS AND ROASTED PINE NUTS

For 6 burgers:

400 g (14 oz/2½ cups) cooked black beans
rapeseed or peanut oil for frying
65 g (2¼ oz/scant ½ cup) finely chopped onion
1 tsp mild chilli powder, e.g. piment d'Espelette
1 tsp smoked paprika powder
3 tbsp BBQ sauce
50 g (2 oz/scant ½ cup) Dry-Roasted Walnuts (see page 149)
2 tbsp finely chopped fresh coriander (cilantro)
100 g (3½ oz/scant ½ cup) boiled black rice
25 g (1 oz/scant ½ cup) panko breadcrumbs
sea salt

To serve:
6 burger buns
butter for the buns
Charcoal-Roasted Baba Ghanoush (see page 124)
Grilled and Steamed Spring Onions (see page 149)
toasted pine nuts
fresh parsley
zest of 1 lemon

Instructions:
1. Rinse the beans in cold water and drain in a colander.
2. Heat a little oil in a frying pan (skillet) and fry the onions over a fairly high heat until they have developed some colour and are on the verge of burning.
3. Reduce the heat, add the chilli and paprika powders and stir. Stir in the BBQ sauce and remove the frying pan from the heat.
4. Roast the walnuts as described on page 149.
5. Chop the walnuts and put them in a bowl together with the beans, coriander, rice, panko breadcrumbs and a pinch of salt. Mix the ingredients together with a potato masher (the beans should only be lightly mashed). Add the onion mixture and stir so that everything is well combined.

6. Take a handful of mixture at a time and shape into 6 round patties, either by hand or using a food ring (see page 10). Put the patties on a large plate and cover with cling film (plastic wrap). Put in the fridge for at least an hour, preferably longer, so that they will hold together better when you fry them.
7. Preheat the oven to 180°C (350°F/Gas 4).
8. Heat a few tablespoons of oil in a frying pan. Fry both sides of the patties over a medium heat for a few minutes. Transfer the patties to an ovenproof dish and bake them in the oven for 5–10 minutes.
9. Butter the buns on the cut surface and fry them quickly in a frying pan or grill (broil) them in the oven.
10. Place a patty on the bottom of each bun. Add a generous dollop of baba ghanoush, follow with some grilled spring onions and top with toasted pine nuts, parsley sprigs and lemon zest.

#06

BABA GHANOUSH AND BORLOTTI BURGER WITH BURRATA AND FRIED TOMATOES

- -

For 6 burgers:

500 g (1 lb 2 oz/2½ cups) cooked borlotti beans
50 g (2 oz/scant ½ cup) Dry-Roasted Walnuts (see page 149)
250 g (9 oz/1 cup) Charcoal-Roasted Baba Ghanoush
  (see page 124)
100 g (3½ oz) Oven-Baked Onions (see page 132)
100 g (3½ oz/scant ½ cup) boiled red rice
25 g (1 oz/scant ½ cup) panko breadcrumbs
sea salt and freshly ground black pepper
rapeseed or peanut oil for frying

Fried tomatoes:
12 cherry tomatoes
olive oil

To serve:
6 burger buns
butter for the buns
burrata
fresh basil
dry-roasted pine nuts
olive oil

Instructions:
1. Rinse the beans in cold water and drain in a colander.
2. Roast the walnuts as described on page 149.
3. Make the baba ghanoush as described on page 124.
4. Bake the onions as described on page 132.
5. Put the oven-baked onions, dry-roasted walnuts and rice into a food processor and mix. Add the baba ghanoush and the panko breadcrumbs and continue mixing until everything is well combined. Add the borlotti beans and pulse-blend for a few seconds.
6. Take a handful of mixture at a time and shape into 6 round patties, either by hand or using a food ring (see page 10). Put them on a plate and cover with cling film (plastic wrap). Put in the fridge for at least an hour,

preferably longer, so they will keep their shape when fried.
7. Preheat the oven to 180°C (350°F/Gas 4).
8. Halve the tomatoes and brush a little oil on the cut surface. Fry the tomatoes in a very hot frying pan (skillet) or chargrill pan for about 5 minutes. Transfer the tomatoes to a bowl and put to one side.
9. Set the hob to a medium heat and pour a little oil into the frying pan. Fry the patties for a few minutes on both sides. Transfer to an ovenproof dish and bake them for 5–10 minutes in the oven.
10. Butter the buns on the cut surface and fry them quickly in a frying pan or grill (broil) them in the oven.
11. Place a patty on each bun, top with grilled tomatoes, a dollop of burrata, basil and pine nuts. Finish by drizzling over a little olive oil.

`Burrata` means 'buttered' in Italian, and developed as a way of using left-over cheese when making mozzarella. Just like classic mozzarella, burrata is made of both buffalo and cow's milk, which then coagulate to form rennet. The cheese mass is subsequently kneaded and rolled out, after which it is filled with pieces of mozzarella and full cream. Everything is then tied together like a bag. Burrata is best if you break it up with your hands and allow the creamy contents to flow out.

- -

07

TWIRLED COURGETTE AND
SWEET POTATO BURGER
WITH CHIPOTLE MAYONNAISE

- -

For 6 burgers:

500 g (1 lb 2 oz) sweet potatoes (2 medium sweet potatoes)
500 g (1 lb 2 oz) courgettes (zucchini) (1–2 courgettes)
50 g (2 oz/¼ cup) butter
sea salt
rapeseed or peanut oil for frying

Oven-baked shallots:
6 shallots
1 tsp red wine vinegar
1 tbsp butter

To serve:
6 burger buns
butter for the buns
tender Swiss chard leaves
Chipotle Mayonnaise (see page 126)

Instructions:
1. Preheat the oven to 180°C (350°F/Gas 4).
2. Peel the sweet potatoes. Shred the courgettes and the sweet potatoes really thinly with a mandoline, preferably using a grating attachment. Put the courgette and sweet potato strips into a bowl.
3. Melt the butter over a low heat. Pour the butter into the bowl of sweet potato and courgette strips. Sprinkle with salt and turn the mixture with a spoon so that everything is well combined.
4. Heat a frying pan (skillet) and pour in a little oil. Twirl up about a sixth of the courgette and sweet potato strips at a time using a fork, put them into a heap in the frying pan and form into small patties. Fry for about 5 minutes on both sides until they start to develop colour and look crispy. If you want you can use a food ring (see page 10) so the patties hold together better, in which case you should put the food ring straight into the frying pan and fill it with courgette and sweet potato strips.
5. Transfer the patties to some paper towel so they release any excess fat. Then put them into an ovenproof dish and finish them off in the oven for 5–10 minutes.
6. Halve the shallots crossways (keeping the skins on). Heat a dry frying pan over a high heat and fry the shallots with the cut surfaces facing downwards so they burn. Then put the shallots into an ovenproof dish with the cut surfaces facing downwards, splash on the vinegar and add the butter. Bake the shallots in the oven for 15 minutes or until they are soft right through. Remove from the oven and push the shallots out of their skins.
7. Butter the buns on the cut surface and fry them quickly in a frying pan or grill (broil) them in the oven.
8. Start off with a little Swiss chard on each bun, place a patty on it, then top with some shallots and a splash of chipotle mayonnaise.

- -

#08

TWIRLED AUBERGINE BURGER WITH HOMEMADE TOMATO KETCHUP AND CARAMELISED ONIONS

For 6 burgers:

800 g (1 lb 12 oz) aubergines (eggplants) (approx. 2 aubergines)
olive oil for frying
200 g (7 oz/scant 1 cup) tomato purée (paste)
2 ×125 g (4 oz) mozzarella balls, coarsely grated
100 g (3½ oz/1 cup) grated Parmesan

Caramelised onions:
2 onions
2 tbsp butter
1 tbsp red wine vinegar

To serve:
6 burger buns
butter for the buns
Pickled Gherkins (see page 136)
Tomato Ketchup (see page 131)

Instructions:
1. Start with the caramelised onions, as they take the longest to prepare: peel and chop the onions and put them in a cold saucepan. Add the butter and put the saucepan on a medium heat. The onions will soon start to release liquid, and the flavours will be concentrated as a result of their cooking in their own juices. Stir with a wooden spoon about every 5 minutes for 30–40 minutes, and check that they're not burning. (If you notice they're starting to get dry you can add the vinegar earlier.)
2. Pour the vinegar into the saucepan of onions, raise the heat and considerably reduce without a lid for 15 minutes. Put to one side.
3. Preheat the oven to 180°C (350°F/Gas 4).
4. Cut the aubergines lengthways into thin slices, ideally using a mandoline. Pour plenty of oil into a frying pan (skillet) and heat until it starts to smoke. Fry the slices of aubergine on both sides so they take on a nice colour, then transfer them to paper towels so they release excess fat.

5. Lay 3–4 slices of aubergine in a row so they form a long strip. Repeat with the remaining slices of aubergine so you get 6 long strips. Spread a thin layer of tomato purée on them and sprinkle grated mozzarella and Parmesan on top. Roll each length up to form a round – as if making a cinnamon roll – of about the same diameter as the bun. Transfer the aubergine rolls to ramekins or heat-resistant teacups. Put in the oven and bake for about 20 minutes. These aubergine patties work best if they are given time to settle, so allow them to cool in the fridge for an hour or so, then reheat them in an oven at 175°C (347°F/Gas 3) for 10 minutes until warmed through.
6. Butter the buns on the cut surface and fry them quickly in a frying pan or grill (broil) them in the oven.
7. Slide a small knife around the edges of the ramekins/teacups, turn them over and slide the aubergine patties out onto a large plate.
8. Carefully place a patty on each bun and top with pickled gherkins, caramelised onion and ketchup.

GRILLED AVOCADO BURGER WITH MARINATED BEANS, CRÈME FRAÎCHE AND FRESH HERBS

For 6 burgers:

3–4 medium avocados
freshly squeezed juice of 1 lime
olive oil

Marinated beans:
200 g (7 oz/1¼ cups) cooked black beans
2–3 Smoked Tomatoes (see page 144)
1 spring onion (scallion), finely chopped
1 tsp finely chopped serrano chilli
1 tbsp finely chopped fresh coriander (cilantro)
1 tsp finely chopped garlic
1 tbsp white wine vinegar
2 tbsp olive oil
zest of 1 lime

To serve:
6 burger buns
butter for the buns
6 tbsp crème fraîche
fresh parsley and coriander (cilantro)
cayenne pepper

Instructions:
1. Rinse the beans and drain them well in a colander.
2. Light the barbecue and make the smoked tomatoes on page 144. You can of course leave the smoking out and use unsmoked tomatoes instead, but the smoky flavour adds a fantastic dimension to the bean mixture. Chop 2–3 tomatoes and mix them and the other ingredients with the marinated beans in a bowl. Stir carefully and put to one side.
3. Halve the avocados and remove the seeds, then carefully scoop out the avocado flesh with a spoon. Cut slices that are as big as possible – about 1 cm (½ in) thick, depending on the size of the avocado. Put the slices on a plate and brush them first with lime juice and then with oil.

4. Grill the avocado slices quickly on the barbecue over a really high heat or burn off the surface with a blowtorch. The surface of the avocado should be caramelised, nearly burnt, while the inside should be cold and retain its consistency.
5. Butter the buns on the cut surface and grill (broil) them quickly on the barbecue.
6. Slap a generous dollop of marinated beans on each bun. Then add 2 slices of avocado, a splash of crème fraîche, a little parsley and coriander. Finish off by sprinkling over a little cayenne pepper.

#10

PULLED SWEET POTATO BURGER WITH FETA CHEESE, MARJORAM AND BLACK VINEGAR MIX

For 6 burgers:

rapeseed oil for frying
6 medium sweet potatoes
6 tbsp coarse sea salt

Black vinegar mix:
1 tsp Roasted Pepper Seasoning (see page 132)
2 spring onions (scallions)
2 tbsp dark malt or red wine vinegar
3 black garlic cloves (see page 156)
sea salt

To serve:
6 burger buns
butter for the buns
300 g (10½ oz) feta
fresh marjoram or oregano

Instructions:
1. Preheat the oven to 200°C (400°F/Gas 6).
2. Make the roasted pepper seasoning for the black vinegar mix as described on page 132.
3. Cut off the green tops of the spring onions. Put the tops on a baking tray lined with baking parchment and grill (broil) them in the oven for about 20 minutes until they are completely black. Thinly slice the white parts of the spring onions and save for the garnish. Put the burnt tops in a blender or food processor and mix to a fine powder. Add the vinegar, black garlic and 1 teaspoon of the roasted pepper seasoning and mix until smooth. Add salt to taste.
4. Heat some oil in a frying pan (skillet) until it starts to smoke. Fry the sweet potatoes all over until the skins are crispy and on the verge of burning. Transfer them to an ovenproof dish, sprinkle sea salt over them and bake for about 45 minutes or until they are completely soft.

5. Split the potatoes lengthways and carefully scoop out the insides with a spoon – try to get everything out in one go so the potato doesn't get mashed. Dicard the skins.
6. Butter the buns on the cut surface and quickly fry them in a frying pan or grill them in the oven.
7. Shape the scooped-out flesh of the sweet potato into 6 round patties, either by hand or using a food ring (see page 10). Place a sweet potato patty on each bun. Brush on the black vinegar mix, crumble over some feta and top off with sliced spring onions and a little fresh marjoram or oregano.

The combination of the tender sweet potatoes and the powerful acidity of the black vinegar mix is a real hit. The black vinegar mix can be used for a lot of things, but is particularly good for counterbalancing raw ingredients that are on the sweet side, e.g. sweet potatoes, parsnips and Jerusalem artichokes.

#11

QUINOA AND SWEET POTATO BURGER WITH HORSERADISH SOUR CREAM, SHALLOTS AND CHIVES

For 6 burgers:

600 g (1 lb 5 oz) sweet potatoes (3 medium sweet potatoes)
2 eggs
100 g (3½ oz/scant 1 cup) chickpea (besan) flour
1 tsp chilli powder, preferably piment d'Espelette
1 tbsp wholegrain Dijon mustard
1 tbsp Walnut Butter or other Nut Butter (see page 149)
juice of ½ lemon
pinch of sea salt
200 g (7 oz/1 cup) boiled quinoa
rapeseed or peanut oil for frying

Horseradish sour cream:
3 tbsp finely grated fresh horseradish
300 g (10½ oz/1¼ cups) sour cream
sea salt

To serve:
6 burger buns
butter for the buns
finely sliced red Asian shallots
finely chopped fresh chives

Instructions:

1. Preheat the oven to 200°C (400°F/Gas 6).

2. Put the sweet potatoes into an ovenproof dish and bake them in the middle of the oven for about 45 minutes or until they are soft all the way through.

3. Split the potatoes lengthways and scoop out the insides with a spoon.

4. Lightly whisk the eggs in a food processor using a knife blade. Add the sweet potatoes, chickpea flour, chilli powder, mustard, nut butter, lemon juice and salt, and pulse-blend until all the ingredients are well combined. Transfer to a bowl and add the quinoa. Turn the mixture with a spoon so that everything is well blended.

5. Take a handful of mixture at a time and shape into 6 round patties, either by hand or using a food ring (see page 10). Put the patties on a plate and cover with cling film (plastic wrap). Put in the fridge for at least an hour, preferably longer, so that the patties will hold together better when you fry them.

6. Preheat the oven to 180°C (350°F/Gas 4).

7. Mix the horseradish and sour cream in a bowl. Add salt to taste and put to one side.

8. Heat a few tablespoons of oil in a frying pan (skillet). Fry both sides of the patties for a few minutes over a medium heat, until they have developed a little colour and a nice surface. Transfer to an ovenproof dish and bake them in the middle of the oven for 5–10 minutes.

9. Butter the buns on the cut surface and fry them quickly in a frying pan or grill (broil) them in the oven.

10. Put a patty at the bottom of each bun, splash on some horseradish sour cream and top with shallots and chives.

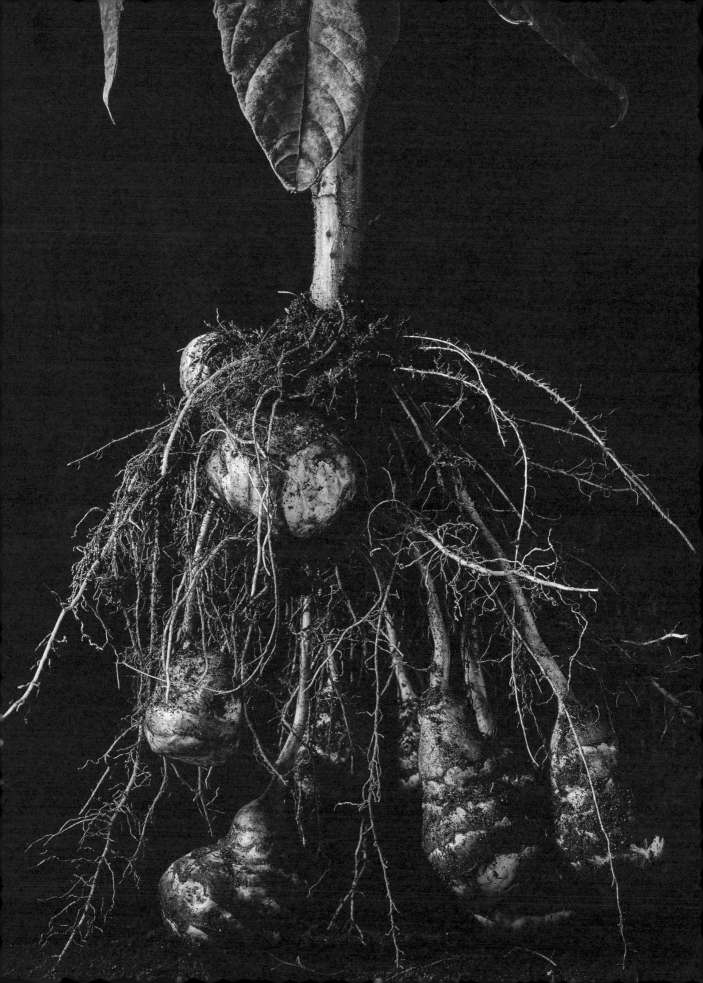

#12

OVEN-BAKED JERUSALEM ARTICHOKE BURGER
WITH CREAMY MISO SAUCE AND
HERB MIX

For 6 burgers:

1 kg (2 lb 3 oz) Jerusalem artichokes (sunchokes)
rapeseed or peanut oil for frying
6 tbsp butter

Herb mix:
2 tbsp finely chopped fresh rosemary
2 tbsp finely chopped fresh thyme
6 tbsp finely chopped fresh parsley
2 tsp crushed green peppercorns
2 tsp white wine vinegar
2 tbsp olive oil
sea salt

Miso sauce:
50 g (2 oz/¼ cup) butter
4 tbsp miso paste
300 ml (10 fl oz/1¼ cups) pouring (whipping) cream

To serve:
6 burger buns
butter for the buns
lettuce leaves

Instructions:

1. Preheat the oven to 200°C (400°F/Gas 6).

2. Mix all the ingredients for the herb mix in a bowl (the mix will be tastiest if you finely chop the herbs instead of mixing them in a blender).

3. Brush the Jerusalem artichokes clean, but retain as much of the skins as possible. I usually use a hard toothbrush to get into all the nooks and crannies. I also cut away the small knotted parts, where there can be a lot of soil.

4. Heat the oil in a frying pan (skillet) until it starts to smoke. Fry the Jerusalem artichokes until the skins are golden brown all over – this takes 10–15 minutes. Transfer the artichokes to a baking tray lined with baking parchment and put in the oven for 10 minutes. Remove from the oven and allow to cool until the artichokes are cool enough to handle.

5. Melt the butter for the miso sauce over a medium heat. Stir in the miso paste. Reduce the heat and whisk in the cream, a little at a time, until you have a glossy, golden brown sauce. Put to one side.

6. Gently bash the Jerusalem artichokes with a spoon so they open up a little. Shape 6 small patties, either by hand or using a food ring (see page 10). Put a knob of butter on each patty. Bake in the oven for a further 10 minutes.

7. Butter the buns on the cut surface and fry them quickly in a frying pan or grill (broil) them in the oven.

8. Put a lettuce leaf at the bottom of each bun. Place á patty on top, spoon over a little miso sauce and finish off with a dash of herb mix.

#13

WHITE BEAN BURGER WITH SMOKED TOMATOES, DEEP-FRIED SAGE AND ROASTED PINE NUTS

For 6 burgers:

3 onions
2 tbsp butter
150 ml (5 fl oz/⅔ cup) white wine
750 g (1 lb 10 oz/4 cups) cooked large white beans
50 g (2 oz/scant 1 cup) panko breadcrumbs
1 tbsp mayonnaise
2 tbsp Cashew Nut Butter or other Nut Butter (see page 149)
2 eggs

Deep-fried sage:

12 sage leaves
peanut oil for frying

To serve:

18 Smoked Tomatoes (see page 144)
6 burger buns
butter for the buns
cos lettuce leaves (romaine)
2 tbsp toasted pine nuts

Instructions:

1. Preheat the oven to 180°C (350°F/Gas 4).

2. Peel and finely chop the onions. Put them in a saucepan with the butter over a medium heat and fry until the onions are soft. Pour over the wine, raise the heat and cook, stirring, until considerably reduced.

3. Rinse the beans in water and drain in a colander.

4. Mix the beans in a food processor or using a hand blender (they should retain a little structure). Put the beans, the reduced onion mixture and the other ingredients for the patties in a bowl. Stir so that everything is well combined.

5. Take a handful of mixture at a time and shape into 6 round patties, either by hand or using a food ring (see page 10). Put the burgers in the fridge for at least an hour, preferably longer, so they hold their shape when fried.

6. Pour plenty of oil into a frying pan (skillet), so it reaches 5 mm–1 cm (¼–½ inch) up the edge. Heat the oil to 180°C (355°F) and deep-fry the sage until it takes on a deep green colour (making sure it doesn't burn). Remove it and drain it on some paper towel.

7. Pour off a little oil from the frying pan, reduce the heat to medium and fry the patties for a few minutes on both sides until they have developed a golden colour and a crispy surface. Transfer them to an ovenproof dish and bake in the oven for 5–10 minutes.

8. Heat the smoked tomatoes in the same frying pan that you fried the burgers in. Pour on a little more oil if necessary. Put to one side and keep warm.

9. Butter the buns on the cut surface and fry them quickly in a frying pan or grill (broil) them in the oven.

10. Put a little lettuce at the bottom of each bun, and top it with a patty, some tomatoes and deep-fried sage leaves. Finish by sprinkling over toasted pine nuts.

Roasting the pine nuts in a dry frying pan brings out the requisite flavour more clearly. But watch out for rancid nuts, which can give rise to so-called pine mouth – a bitter aftertaste that can ruin your sense of taste for several days.

#14

BBQ PORTOBELLO BURGER WITH CARAMELISED ONIONS AND SAINT AGUR CHEESE

- -

For 6 burgers:

4 Grilled and Steamed Spring Onions (see page 149)
600 g (1 lb 5 oz) portobello mushrooms
rapeseed or peanut oil for frying
2 finely chopped garlic cloves
1 tbsp butter
100 g (3½ oz) day-old sourdough bread, finely chopped
300 ml (10 fl oz) BBQ sauce
2 eggs

Caramelised onions:

2 onions
2 tbsp butter
1 tbsp red wine vinegar

To serve:

120 g (4 oz) Saint Agur or other creamy blue cheese
6 burger buns
butter for the buns
finely chopped fresh chives, preferably garlic chives with flowers

Instructions:

1. Grill and steam the spring onions as described on page 149.

2. Cut the mushrooms into 5 mm (¼ in) cubes. Heat the oil in a frying pan (skillet) over a high heat until it starts to smoke. Add the mushrooms and fry them so that they take on colour – for 10–15 minutes.

3. Chop the steamed spring onions and add them and the garlic to the mushrooms in the pan. Add the butter, reduce the heat to medium and cook for a few minutes, stirring.

4. Remove the frying pan from the heat and allow it to cool a little. Then add the bread, BBQ sauce and eggs. Stir so that everything is well combined.

5. Take a handful of mixture at a time and shape into 6 round patties, either by hand or using a food ring (see page 10). Put the patties in the fridge for at least an hour, preferably longer, then they will hold together better when you fry them.

6. Peel and chop the onions for the caramelised onion mix. Put the chopped onions and the butter into a cold saucepan. Cook over a medium heat and put the lid on. The onions will soon start to release liquid, and the flavours will be concentrated as a result of their cooking in their own juices. Stir with a wooden spoon about once every 5 minutes for 30–40 minutes, and check that they are not burning. (If you notice they're starting to get too dry you can add the vinegar earlier.)

7. Pour on the vinegar, increase the heat and cook for about 15 minutes, stirring, until considerably reduced. Put to one side.

8. Preheat the oven to 180°C (350°F/Gas 4) using the grill (broiler) function.

9. Heat up a few tablespoons of oil in a frying pan over a medium heat. Fry the patties for a few minutes on both sides, until they develop a nice colour and a crispy surface. Transfer to an ovenproof dish and grill (broil) in the oven for 5–10 minutes.

10. Put a little cheese on each patty and cook for a little longer in the oven, until the cheese has melted. This won't take long, so keep an eye on them!

11. Butter the buns on the cut surface and fry them quickly in a frying pan or grill them in the oven.

12. Place a patty on the bottom of each bun. Splash on a heaped spoonful of the onion mix and top with chives.

#15

CHICKPEA AND GRILLED PEPPER BURGER WITH DILL-DUNKED CUCUMBER SALAD

For 6 burgers:

3 red (bell) peppers
olive oil
sea salt and freshly ground black pepper
200 g (7 oz) Oven-Baked Onions (see page 132)
500 g (1 lb 2 oz/3 cups) cooked chickpeas
3 garlic cloves
2 eggs
1 tbsp smoked paprika
1 tbsp mild chilli powder, e.g. piment d'Espelette
50 g (2 oz/scant 1 cup) panko breadcrumbs
rapeseed or peanut oil for frying

Cucumber salad:
1 bunch of dill + a few dill heads as necessary
2 cucumbers
zest of 1 lemon
sesame seeds
olive oil
sea salt and freshly ground black pepper

To serve:
6 burger buns
butter for the buns

Instructions:
1. Preheat the grill (broiler) to 250°C (475°F/Gas 7).
2. Halve the peppers and remove the core and seeds. Put the pepper halves on a baking tray with the skins facing up and drizzle oil over them. Sprinkle with salt and black pepper. Grill (broil) until the skin is black. Remove the peppers and transfer to a plastic bag. Allow them to cool, then rub or pull off the skin and cut into pieces.
3. Make the oven-baked onions on page 132.

4. Rinse the chickpeas in cold water and drain them well in a colander.
5. Peel and finely chop the garlic. Lightly whisk the eggs in a food processor. Add the oven-baked onions, chickpeas, grilled peppers, paprika powder, chilli powder, panko breadcrumbs, garlic and salt. Pulse-blend so all the ingredients are well combined, but not too finely blended.
6. Take a handful of mixture at a time and shape into 6 round patties, either by hand or using a food ring (see page 10). Put the patties in the fridge for at least an hour, preferably longer, so that they hold together better when you fry them.
7. Preheat the oven to 180°C (350°F/Gas 4).
8. Take some sprigs of dill for the cucumber salad. Shave the cucumber for the salad lengthways using a vegetable peeler (see photo on previous page). If you want you can first remove the seeds from the middle – the cucumber will release less water. Put the cucumber slices in a bowl and mix in the dill, lemon zest and sesame seeds, and some dill heads. Drizzle over a little olive oil and carefully turn the salad using your hands. (Avoid using any implements, otherwise the cucumber may get squeezed to pieces.) Season to taste.
9. Heat a frying pan (skillet) over a medium heat and pour in a little oil. Fry the patties for a few minutes on both sides, until they have a nice colour and a crispy surface. Transfer the patties to an ovenproof dish and bake for 5–10 minutes.
10. Butter the buns on the cut surface and fry them quickly in a frying pan or grill them in the oven.
11. Put a patty at the bottom of each bun and top with the cucumber salad, and a few dill heads, if you like.

The chickpeas and (bell) peppers in Burger No. 15 go amazingly well together, in both flavour and consistency. The crispy chickpeas perfectly contrast with the grilled peppers' smooth, almost meaty consistency. How much spice you add in the form of chilli and paprika is a matter of individual taste – but personally I think that this patty can cope with a lot of heat, and that the heat further emphasises the sweet and sour taste of the peppers.

#16

BBQ PORTOBELLO BURGER
WITH GRILLED PEPPERS
AND MAYONNAISE

For 6 burgers:

4 Grilled and Steamed Spring Onions (see page 149)
600 g (1 lb 5 oz) portobello mushrooms
rapeseed or peanut oil for frying
2 finely chopped garlic cloves
1 tbsp butter
100 g (3½ oz) finely chopped day-old sourdough bread
300 ml (10 fl oz) BBQ sauce
2 eggs
pinch of sea salt

To serve:

2–3 red (bell) peppers
6 burger buns
butter for the buns
lettuce leaves
600 g (1 lb 5 oz/2½ cups) Basic Mayonnaise (see page 126)
fresh herbs, e.g. marjoram, oregano and thyme

Instructions:

1. Grill and steam the spring onions as described on page 149.

2. Cut the mushrooms into 5 mm (¼ in) cubes. Heat the oil in a frying pan (skillet) over a high heat until it starts to smoke. Add the mushrooms and fry them for 10–15 minutes so they develop some colour.

3. Chop the steamed spring onions, and, together with the garlic, add them to the mushrooms in the pan. Add the butter and reduce the heat to medium. Fry for a few minutes while stirring.

4. Remove the frying pan from the heat and transfer the mushroom mixture to a bowl. Allow it to cool.

5. Add the finely chopped bread, BBQ sauce and eggs to the mushrooms in the bowl. Stir so that all the ingredients are well combined, and add a little salt to taste.

6. Take a handful of mixture at a time and shape into 6 round patties, either by hand or using a food ring (see page 10). Put the burgers in the fridge for at least an hour, preferably longer, then they will hold together better when you fry them.

7. Preheat the oven to 180°C (350°F/Gas 4).

8. Light the barbecue and grill the peppers well all over so they go black on the outside. I usually add the peppers while the fuel is still actively flaming – ideally over a wood fire. (You can also grill (broil) the peppers in the oven on maximum heat until they are almost completely black.) Transfer the peppers ino a plastic bag and let them cool for about 10 minutes. Then rub off the skin by massaging them while they are still in the bag. Cut the peppers into equal-sized pieces.

9. Take the portobello patties from the fridge and brush them with oil. Fry them in a frying pan for a few minutes on both sides so they develop a nice colour and a crispy surface. Transfer to an ovenproof dish and bake them in the oven for 10 minutes.

10. Butter the buns on the cut surface and fry them quickly in a frying pan or grill them in the oven.

11. Place a patty on the bottom of each bun. Put a lettuce leaf, some pieces of grilled pepper and a generous splash of mayonnaise on top. Finish off with fresh herbs.

#17

BRUSSELS SPROUTS AND PURPLE POTATO BURGER WITH PICKLED RED ONIONS AND CRESS

For 4 burgers:

50–75 g (2–2½ oz/¼ cup) butter
8 firm purple potatoes, such as Blue Congo
16 medium Brussels sprouts
sea salt and freshly ground black pepper
rapeseed or peanut oil for frying

To serve:
4 burger buns
butter for the buns
Pickled Red Onions (see page 136)
garden cress

Instructions:

1. Preheat the oven to 180°C (350°F/Gas 4).

2. Melt the butter in a saucepan over a low heat. Put to one side and allow it to cool.

3. Scrub the potatoes, then dry them thoroughly. Shred them very thinly with a mandoline, preferably using a grating attachment. Finely slice the Brussels sprouts crossways, working from the top down towards the root.

4. Put the potato shreds and sprout slices into a bowl. Pour over the melted butter. Sprinkle with salt and pepper. Mix carefully with your hands, so the butter is evenly distributed over the potatoes and sprouts. The potatoes will also release starch, making it easier to form patties.

5. Shape 8 patties from the butter-dunked potato and sprout mixture, preferably using a food ring to shape nice round patties (see page 10).

6. Heat the oil in a frying pan (skillet) until it starts to smoke. Reduce the heat and carefully lay two patties at a time in the pan. Fry for about 5 minutes on both sides. Avoid moving them around too much with the spatula, otherwise there is a risk that they will fall apart. If they start to break apart you can carefully press back the edges using a spatula.

7. Place the patties on a plate lined with paper towel so they release excess fat, then transfer them to an ovenproof dish and bake them for about 10 minutes.

8. Butter the buns on the cut surface and fry them quickly in a frying pan or grill (broil) them in the oven.

9. Put 2 patties on each bun and top with pickled red onions and cress.

#18

ROASTED CELERIAC BURGER WITH HERB CREAM AND CHANTERELLES

- -

For 6 burgers:

3 small celeriacs (celery roots) (the diameter should correspond to the size of the bun)
rapeseed or peanut oil for frying
sea salt and freshly ground black pepper

Herb cream:

1 bunch of mixed fresh herbs, e.g. thyme, rosemary and dill
freshly squeezed juice of ½ lemon
3 tbsp olive oil
sea salt and freshly ground black pepper
100 g (3½ oz/scant ½ cup) crème fraîche

Chanterelles fried in butter:

rapeseed or peanut oil for frying
150–200 g (5–7 oz) chanterelles
2–3 garlic cloves
2 tbsp butter
sea salt and freshly ground black pepper

To serve:

6 burger buns
butter for the buns
fresh dill and thyme

Instructions:

1. Preheat the oven to 180°C (350°F/Gas 4).

2. Scrub the celeriacs clean under running water. Then fully dry them.

3. Heat plenty of oil in a frying pan (skillet) and flash-fry the celeriacs all over until the skin is golden brown (do not cut them up). Transfer them to an ovenproof dish and sprinkle with salt and pepper. Bake for about 2 hours, or until they are soft on the inside.

4. For the herb cream, mix together the herbs, lemon juice and olive oil using a hand blender or food processor. Add salt and pepper to taste. Pour the crème fraîche into a bowl and sprinkle the herb mixture over it, while carefully stirring with a fork so as to create a delicate marbling on the surface. Put to one side.

5. For the chanterelles, heat the oil in a frying pan until it starts to smoke. Toss in the chanterelles and flash-fry them for a minute or so. Peel the garlic cloves, crush them with the thick edge of a knife and put them in the pan together with the butter. Reduce the heat and fry until the mushrooms develop a nice colour.

6. Butter the buns on the cut surface and fry them quickly in a frying pan or grill (broil) them in the oven.

7. Cut the roasted celeriac into 1 cm- (½ in-) thick slices and put 2–3 slices on each bun. Splash on a little herb cream, put a fistful of mushrooms on top and finish off with fresh herbs.

#19

BEER-MARINATED AUBERGINE BURGER WITH MISO-FRIED CARROTS AND DEEP-FRIED SAGE

For 6 burgers:

2–3 large aubergines (eggplants)

Marinade:
330 ml (11 fl oz) beer, such as brown ale
2 lightly crushed garlic cloves
2 tbsp malt vinegar
2 sprigs of fresh thyme (save a little for a garnish)
2 sprigs of fresh lovage or parsley
2 tsp sea salt

Dressing:
1 vanilla bean
4 tbsp olive oil
2 tbsp apple cider vinegar
2 black garlic cloves (see page 156)
1 tbsp honey
sea salt and pink pepper

Deep-fried sage:
fresh sage leaves (2–4 leaves per burger)
peanut oil for frying

Miso-fried carrots:
2 carrots
2 tbsp miso paste
peanut oil for deep-frying

To serve:
6 burger buns
butter for the buns

Instructions:

1. Cut the aubergines into 1–1.5 cm (½ in) slices (try to make the pieces as evenly sized as possible). Put the ingredients for the marinade in a plastic bag and add the aubergine slices. Rub the aubergine through the bag so that the marinade is evenly distributed. Leave the aubergines to marinate for 7–8 hours in the fridge. Shake the bag and rub the aubergines occasionally.

2. Light the barbecue or preheat the oven to 200°C (400°F/Gas 6).

3. Remove the aubergine slices from the marinade. Place them on paper towels and thoroughly dry the cut surfaces. Grill the slices until they develop a golden colour and surface, or roast them for about 20 minutes.

4. Cut the vanilla bean lengthways and scrape out the seeds. Put the vanilla seeds and the other ingredients for the dressing into a bowl and mix using a hand blender. Put to one side.

5. Using a mandoline, thinly cut the carrots into slices about 2 mm (⅛ in) thick.

6. Pour plenty of the oil into a frying pan (skillet), so it reaches 5 mm–1 cm (¼–½ in) up the edge. Heat the oil to 180°C (355°F) and deep-fry the sage until it goes deep green (making sure it doesn't burn). Remove it and drain on paper towels.

7. Put the carrots in the frying pan you fried the sage in and lightly deep-fry them, for about 1 minute on both sides. Remove and drain on paper towels.

8. Pour off most of the oil, but save about 2 tablespoons. Add the miso paste and dissolve it in the oil. Put the carrots back in again and continue frying them until they are crispy and golden brown – on the verge of being dark brown. Transfer to a colander and drain.

9. Butter the buns on the cut surface and fry them quickly in a frying pan or grill (broil) them in the oven.

10. Place 2 slices of aubergine on the bottom of each bun, put some carrots on top, drizzle over the dressing and top off with the deep-fried sage leaves and a little thyme.

#20

AFRICAN WEST COAST BURGER
WITH DEEP-FRIED PLANTAIN
AND CRUSHED PEANUTS

For 6 burgers:

200 g (7 oz) Oven-Baked Onions (see page 132)
500 g (1 lb 2 oz/2½ cups) cooked kidney beans
3 tbsp peanut butter
150 g (5 oz/generous ¾ cup) boiled long-grain rice
300 g (10½ oz) fresh spinach, roughly chopped
150 g (5 oz) okra, roughly chopped (frozen is fine)
2 tbsp finely chopped jalapeño chilli

Deep-fried plantain:

300 g (10½ oz) plantain (cooking banana)
1 litre (34 fl oz/4 cups) peanut oil
sea salt

To serve:
6 burger buns
butter for the buns
120 g (4 oz) unsalted peanuts, crushed
Tomato Ketchup (see page 131)

Instructions:
1. Make the oven-baked onions as described on page 132.
2. Rinse the beans in cold water and drain in a colander.
3. Put the oven-baked onions, peanut butter and rice into a food processor and mix. Add the beans and pulse-blend quickly so the beans are broken up a little. Transfer to a bowl and add the spinach, okra and jalapeño. Turn the mixture with a ladle so everything is well combined.
4. Take a handful of mixture at a time and shape into 6 round patties, either by hand or using a food ring (see page 10). Put the patties on a plate and cover with cling film (plastic wrap). Put them in the fridge for at least an hour, preferably longer, so that the patties will hold together better when you fry them.
5. Preheat the oven to 180°C (350°F/Gas 4).
6. Cut the plantain diagonally into 1 cm- (½ in-) thick slices.

Heat the oil to 180°C (355°F) in a high-sided saucepan. Reduce the heat to medium, then try to keep the temperature at 180°C (355°F) as far as possible. Deep-fry the plantain slices for 2–3 minutes, until they have developed a golden colour, pushing them round with a slotted spoon. Remove the plantain and put it on a plate lined with paper towel so that excess fat is absorbed. Sprinkle with salt on both sides.
7. Heat a little of the peanut oil from the deep-frying in a frying pan (skillet). Fry the patties over a medium heat for a few minutes on both sides so they develop a nice colour. Transfer them to an ovenproof dish and bake in the oven for 5–10 minutes.
8. Butter the buns on the cut surface and fry them quickly in a frying pan or grill (broil) them in the oven.
9. Place a patty on the bottom of each bun. Put some slices of deep-fried plantain on top and finish with peanuts and ketchup.

When I was in Sierra Leone I used to eat plantain - usually deep-fried - with most things. Plantain is extremely rich in starch and works well deep-fried. It's tastiest when it's still green (otherwise it gets too sweet). In this recipe I use it as a topping for the burger, but it's equally suitable as an accompaniment instead of chips.

#21

PANKO-CRUSTED DEEP-FRIED KING OYSTER MUSHROOM BURGER WITH COURGETTE KIMCHI

- -

For 6 burgers:

2 onions
2 tbsp butter
1 tbsp sherry vinegar
1 tbsp soy sauce
1 tsp sesame oil
1 tbsp finely chopped dried shiitake mushrooms
600 g (1 lb 5 oz) king oyster (eryngii) mushrooms
2 tbsp rapeseed oil
100 g (3½ oz/1¾ cups) panko breadcrumbs
3 eggs
90–120 g (3¼–4 oz/approx. ¾ cup) plain (all-purpose) flour
1 litre (34 fl oz/4 cups) peanut oil
sea salt

To serve:
6 burger buns
butter for the buns
lettuce leaves
Courgette Kimchi (see page 140)
spring onions (scallions)
finely sliced chilli

Instructions:

1. Peel and chop the onions and put them in a cold saucepan together with the butter. Put the saucepan on a medium heat and put the lid on. The onions will soon start to release liquid, and the flavours will be concentrated as a result of their cooking in their own juices. Stir with a wooden spoon once every 5 minutes for 30–40 minutes, and check that they're not burning. (If you notice they're starting to get too dry you can add the vinegar earlier.)

2. Add the vinegar, soy sauce, sesame oil and dried shiitake mushrooms to the onions in the saucepan. Raise the heat and cook for about 15 minutes until considerably reduced. Take the saucepan off the heat and put to one side.

3. Cut the oyster mushrooms into 5 mm (¼ in) cubes. Heat the rapeseed oil in a frying pan (skillet) until it starts to smoke. Add the mushrooms and flash-fry them so they develop some colour. Then remove the frying pan from the heat and allow to cool.

4. Stir together the fried oyster mushrooms, onion mix and 2 tablespoons of the panko breadcrumbs in a bowl and mix together well.

5. Take a handful of mixture at a time and shape into 6 round patties, either by hand or using a food ring (see page 10). Put the patties on a plate and cover with cling film (plastic wrap). Leave in the freezer until frozen through.

6. Preheat the oven to 200°C (400°F/Gas 6).

7. Break the eggs into a bowl and lightly whisk them. Pour the flour and remaining panko breadcrumbs into separate bowls and place the bowls in a row near to the cooker.

8. Fill a high-sided saucepan with the peanut oil and place on the hob. Heat the oil to 190°C (375°F), then reduce the setting to medium and try to keep the oil at 190°C (375°F) as far as possible.

9. Remove the oyster mushroom patties from the freezer and dip them first in the flour, then in the whisked egg and finally in the panko breadcrumbs. Deep-fry 2 patties at a time in the oil for 2–3 minutes on both sides so they develop a golden-brown colour, pushing them around with a slotted spoon.

10. Lift the patties out and drain on paper towel. Sprinkle with salt on both sides. Transfer them to an ovenproof dish and bake them in the oven for 5–10 minutes.

11. Shred the green parts of the spring onions.

12. Butter the buns on the cut surface and fry them quickly in a frying pan or grill (broil) them in the oven.

13. Put a little lettuce at the bottom of each bun. Place a patty on top, spoon over some courgette kimchi and finish off with spring onions and chilli.

- -

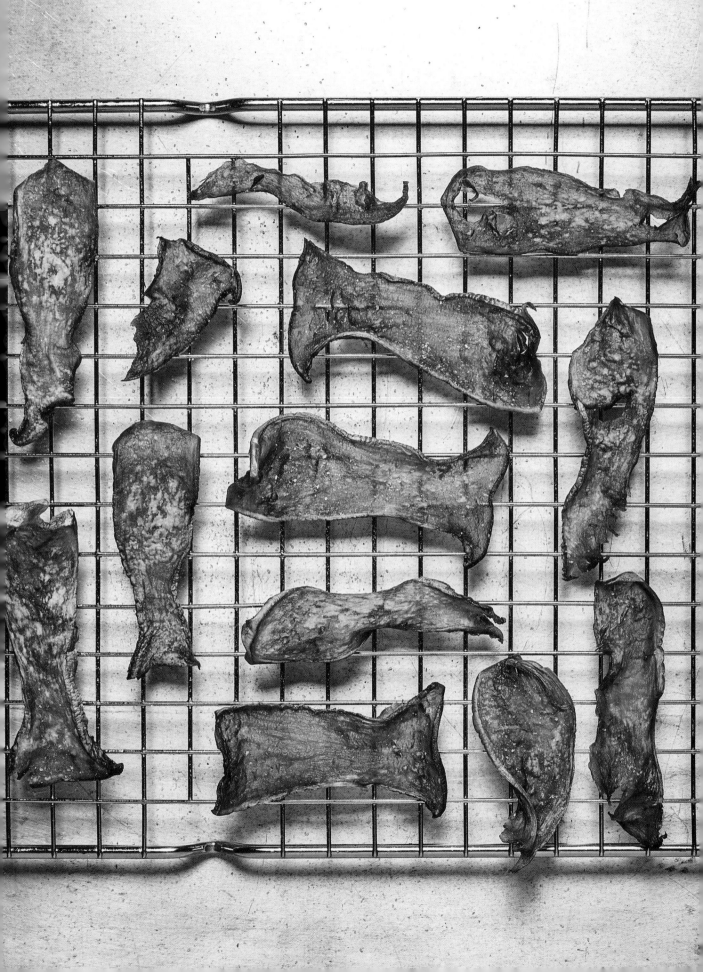

#22

PEA BURGER WITH CREAM CHEESE MIX AND KING OYSTER CRISPS

For 6 burgers:

200 g (7 oz) Oven-Baked Onions (see page 132)
30 g (1 oz) fresh mint + a few leaves to garnish
15 g (½ oz) fresh lovage
2–3 eggs
50 g (2 oz/scant 1 cup) panko breadcrumbs
800 g (1 lb 12 oz) peas (cooked and cooled,
    or thawed frozen ones)
4 garlic cloves
4 spring onions (scallions)
rapeseed or peanut oil for frying

Cream cheese mix:

120 g (4 oz) cream cheese
2 tbsp finely chopped garlic
sea salt and pink pepper

King oyster crisps:

2–3 king oyster (eryngii) mushrooms
1 litre (34 fl oz/4 cups) peanut or other deep-frying oil
sea salt

To serve:

6 burger buns
butter for the buns
crushed pink peppercorns

Instructions:

1. Make the oven-baked onions according to the recipe on page 132.

2. Put the oven-baked onions, mint and lovage in a food processor and mix until everything is finely distributed. Add the eggs and panko breadcrumbs and mix until well combined. Finally, add the peas and pulse-blend or mix quickly for a few seconds so the peas break up a little.

3. Peel the garlic. Finely chop the garlic and spring onions and stir them into the pea mixture.

4. Take a handful of mixture at a time and shape into 6 round patties, either by hand or using a food ring (see page 10). Put the patties on a plate and cover with cling film (plastic wrap). Put in the fridge for at least an hour, preferably longer, so that they will hold together better when you fry them.

5. Preheat the oven to 180°C (350°F/Gas 4).

6. Mix the cream cheese with the garlic in a bowl. Add salt and pink pepper to taste.

7. For the crisps, thinly slice the mushrooms. Heat the oil to about 180°C (355°F) in a high-sided saucepan. Add the slices of mushroom and deep-fry them until they are golden brown, pushing them around with a slotted spoon. Remove the mushroom crisps and drain on paper towel. Sprinkle with salt on both sides.

8. Heat a few tablespoons of oil in a frying pan (skillet). Fry the patties over a medium heat for a few minutes on both sides, until they have developed a nice colour. Transfer them to an ovenproof dish and bake in the oven for about 5–10 minutes.

9. Butter the buns on the cut surface and fry them quickly in a frying pan or grill (broil) them in the oven.

10. Place a patty on the bottom of each bun. Put a generous dollop of cream cheese mix and some oyster mushroom crisps on top, finishing off with mint leaves and a little crushed pink pepper.

#23

GRILLED PORTOBELLO BURGER WITH ROASTED KALE, CONFIT PEPPERS AND SAINT AGUR CHEESE

For 6 burgers:

2 garlic cloves
50 g (2 oz/¼ cup) butter
fresh thyme
6 large portobello mushrooms
sea salt and freshly ground black pepper

Confit peppers:
2–3 red (bell) peppers
500–600 ml (17–20 fl oz/2–2½ cups) olive oil
8 garlic cloves, peeled
3 ancho chillies
zest of 1 lemon
1 tsp coriander seeds
1 tsp whole black peppercorns
fresh oregano

To serve:
6 burger buns
butter for the buns
100 g (3½ oz) Saint Agur cheese or other creamy blue cheese
Roasted Kale (see page 147)
fresh thyme

Instructions:
1. Make the confit peppers. Cut the peppers into 3 x 2 cm (1¼ x ¾ in) pieces. Pour the oil into a high-sided saucepan. Put the saucepan over a low heat and add the pieces of pepper a few at a time, so they are fully immersed in the oil. Simmer carefully for 5–10 minutes until the peppers start to soften. If you wish, you can also add the garlic and ancho chillies for a few minutes at the end.

2. Transfer the pieces of pepper to a sterilised jar as they become ready. Add the other ingredients to the confit peppers and finish by pouring over the oil from the pan. Allow to cool, put the lid on and store the jar in the fridge. The pepper can be served cold, or you can heat them up in a frying pan (skillet) immediately before serving.
3. For the patties, gently crush the 2 garlic cloves with the flat of a knife (keeping the skin on). Melt the butter in a saucepan together with the garlic and thyme sprigs (save a few leaves for a garnish), then remove the saucepan from the heat.
4. Remove and discard the stems of the portobello mushrooms and cut the mushrooms into 5 mm- (¼ in-) thick slices.
5. Light the barbecue and wait until it is glowing (you can also fry the mushrooms in a frying pan). Grill the mushrooms until they start to shrink and develop a little colour. Brush on a little of the melted butter and turn them over. Repeat this a few times until the mushrooms are golden brown and have developed a nice surface. Sprinkle with salt and pepper.
6. Butter the buns on the cut surface and grill (broil) or fry them quickly in a frying pan.
7. Put some slices of portobello mushroom at the bottom of each bun. Crumble over the cheese and put a few pieces of confit pepper and some roasted kale on top. Finish off by sprinkling over a little thyme.

24

SEARED TOFU BURGER WITH PICKLED RADISHES, BLACKENED MAYONNAISE AND FRIED EGG

- -

For 6 burgers:

600 g (1 lb 5 oz) firm tofu
butter for frying
6 eggs

To serve:
6 Pickled Radishes (see page 137)
fresh coriander (cilantro) leaves or roots
6 burger buns
butter for the buns
300 g (10½ oz) Classic Kimchi (see page 143)
6 tbsp Blackened Mayonnaise (see page 128)

Instructions:
1. Cut the tofu into 6 slices, then halve each slice.
2. Put a dry frying pan (skillet) over a very high heat and wait until it is really hot. Place one slice of tofu at a time in the pan and gently press it down with a spatula. Fry the tofu quickly until the surface is blackened. The tofu must keep its cold, silky-smooth consistency inside, so it is important that you do not fry it for long. Remove and set aside.
3. Heat some butter in the frying pan. Fry the eggs carefully over a medium heat – the yolk must stay runny.
4. Thinly cut the pickled radishes and pick the coriander leaves or thinly shred the coriander roots.
5. Butter the buns on the cut surface and fry them quickly in a frying pan or grill (broil) them in the oven.
6. Place 2 slices of tofu at the bottom of each bun. Put a generous serving of kimchi, a dash of mayonnaise and some pickled radishes on top. Finish off with a fried egg and coriander leaves or shredded coriander roots.

- -

#25

BUTTER-ROASTED CAULIFLOWER BURGER WITH GOAT'S CHEESE CREAM, LEMON OIL AND PINK PEPPER

- -

For 6 burgers:

*3 small cauliflower heads (the diameter must
    correspond to the size of the bun)*
150 g (5 oz/⅔ cup) butter at room temperature
sea salt and freshly ground black pepper

Lemon oil:
shaved peel of ½ lemon
100 ml (3½ fl oz/scant ½ cup) olive oil

Goat's cheese cream:
*200 g (7 oz) creamy Norwegian goat's cheese
    (preferably truffle-flavoured) or feta*
200 g (7 oz/generous ¾ cup) crème fraîche
sea salt

To serve:
6 burger buns
butter for the buns
1 tbsp coarsely crushed pink peppercorns
watercress
zest of ½ lemon

Instructions:

1. Preheat the oven to 200°C (400°F/Gas 6).

2. For the lemon oil, heat the lemon peel and olive oil in a small saucepan. Remove the saucepan from the hob when it starts to simmer and leave for about 10 minutes so the oil takes on the flavour of the lemon, then remove the lemon peel and put the oil to one side.

3. Trim the heads of cauliflower and rub in plenty of butter. Sprinkle with salt and pepper. Transfer them to an ovenproof dish and bake for 10 minutes in the middle of the oven. Then reduce the heat to 150°C (300°F/Gas 2) and bake for a further 30–40 minutes, until the cauliflower has taken on a golden colour and starts to soften. The florets should give if you press them gently, but they must not go too soft, otherwise the cauliflower won't hold together when you cut it up.

4. Put the goat's cheese into a bowl and mash it with a fork. Add the crème fraîche and stir to make a smooth cream. Add salt to taste.

5. Butter the buns on the cut surface and fry them quickly in a frying pan (skillet) or grill (broil) them in the oven.

6. Cut the cauliflower into 1 cm- (½ in-) thick slices and place two slices on each bun. Spread on a little of the goat's cheese cream, sprinkle over some crushed pink pepper and add a little watercress. Drizzle lemon oil over it and finish by topping with a little lemon zest.

Cauliflower is just amazing! Just as with all brassicas you can do so much with it, but the best thing is to roast it or fry it in butter. When the delicious butter is absorbed into the crispy surface of the cauliflower and then reaches the soft flesh, the result is magical.

- -

Charcoal grilling of root vegetables creates an incredibly intense and delicious flavour, and is also pretty easy. I usually chuck the root vegetables straight onto the charcoal while it is still actively flaming. When the surface is practically charred I remove them and let them cool. Make sure you use charcoal or wood that has not been chemically treated. The very best way is of course direct roasting in a wood fire.

#26

LENTIL AND CHARCOAL-ROASTED CARROT BURGER WITH ROASTED KALE AND GREEN BANANA GUACAMOLE

For 6 burgers:

250 g (9 oz) Oven-Baked Onions (see page 132)
2 tbsp Dry-Roasted Walnuts (see page 149)
500 g (1 lb 2 oz) thick carrots
60 g (2 oz) day-old bread, broken into pieces
1 bunch of fresh coriander (cilantro)
2 tsp mild chilli powder, e.g. piment d'Espelette
juice of 1 lemon
120 g (4 oz/1½ cups) cooked red lentils
rapeseed or peanut oil for frying

To serve:
6 burger buns
butter for the buns
Roasted Kale (see page 147)
Green Banana Guacamole (see page 135)
thinly sliced jalapeño

Instructions:

1. Make the oven-baked onions as described on page 132.
2. Roast the walnuts as described on page 149.
3. Light the barbecue. Make sure you use charcoal that has not been chemically treated. Put the carrots straight onto the charcoal – you can do this when the charcoal is actively flaming – and roast the carrots for 30–40 minutes, until they are completely black. Remove them with barbecue tongs and allow to cool.
4. Rub the skin off the carrots, either wearing rubber gloves or using a plastic bag. Divide the carrots into small pieces.
5. Put the carrots, oven-baked onions, 2 tablespoons of dry-roasted walnuts, bread, coriander, chilli powder and lemon juice into a food processor and mix to form an even consistency. Transfer to a bowl and stir in the red lentils.

6. Take a handful of mixture at a time and shape into 6 round patties, either by hand or using a food ring (see page 10). Put the patties on a plate and cover with cling film (plastic wrap). Put in the fridge for at least an hour, preferably longer, then they will hold together better when you fry them.
7. Preheat the oven to 180°C (350°F/Gas 4).
8. Heat some oil in a frying pan (skillet). Fry the patties over a medium heat for about 5 minutes on both sides. Transfer them to an ovenproof dish and bake them in the oven for 5–10 minutes.
9. Butter the buns on the cut surface and fry them quickly in a frying pan or grill (broil) them in the oven.
10. Put a little roasted kale on the bottom of each bun. Place a patty on top and finish with the green banana guacamole and jalapeño slices.

27

GRILLED HALLOUMI BURGER
WITH ONION-AND-MUSHROOM MIX
TOPPED WITH FRESH THYME

For 6 burgers:

3 x 200 g (7 oz) packs of halloumi

Onion and mushroom mix:
1 tsp Roasted Pepper Seasoning (see page 132)
2 onions
2 tbsp butter
1 tbsp dark balsamic vinegar
250 g (9 oz) baby portobello or field mushrooms
rapeseed or peanut oil for frying
sea salt and freshly ground black pepper
2 egg yolks

To serve:
6 burger buns
butter for the buns
fresh thyme

Instructions:
1. Make the roasted pepper seasoning as described on page 132.
2. Peel and chop the onions. Put the onions and the butter in a cold saucepan. Place the saucepan over a medium heat and put the lid on. The onions will soon start to release liquid, and the flavours will be concentrated as a result of their cooking in their own juices. Stir with a wooden spoon about once every 5 minutes for 30–40 minutes, and check that they're not burning. (If you notice they're starting to get dry you can add the vinegar earlier.)
3. Remove the lid, pour on the vinegar and increase the heat. Cook for about 15 minutes, stirring, until you have a sticky onion mix. Put the pan to one side.
4. Brush the mushrooms with a little oil. Sprinkle with salt and pepper. Cook the mushrooms in a frying pan (skillet) – it doesn't matter if they get a little burnt – then cut the mushrooms up into pieces the same size as the onions.

5. Put the mushrooms in a bowl together with the onion mix. Stir in the egg yolks and season with 1 teaspoon of roasted pepper seasoning.
6. Light the barbecue (if you want to barbecue).
7. Rinse the halloumi if necessary and dry it off using paper towel (personally I find halloumi a little too salty, so I always rinse it before cooking). Slice it and fry or grill (broil) it immediately before the burgers are to be served.
8. Butter the buns on the cut surface and grill carefully on the barbecue or fry them quickly in a frying pan.
9. Place some slices of halloumi on the bottom of each bun. Spoon over a generous amount of onion and mushroom mix and finish by sprinkling over a little fresh thyme.

When I chop onions that are to be caramelised, I first cut off the roots and tops, then halve them lengthways, from root to top. I then peel them, and slice them up in the same direction. When you slice in this way you cut against the onion's cell structure, and the onions will break down faster when you fry them. You thus get a softer and creamier result.

#28

BEETROOT BURGER
WITH PEA HUMMUS
AND PEA SHOOTS

For 6 burgers:

500 g (1 lb 2 oz) beetroots (beets)
2–3 tbsp olive oil
coarse sea salt
6–7 garlic cloves
fresh oregano
1 tsp Roasted Pepper Seasoning (see page 132)
120 g (4 oz/⅔ cup) boiled red rice
25 g (1 oz/scant ½ cup) panko breadcrumbs
2 tbsp Almond Butter or other Nut Butter (see page 149)
150 g (5 oz/⅔ cup) cooked red lentils
100 g (3½ oz/scant ½ cup) cooked red quinoa
a pinch of sea salt as necessary
rapeseed or peanut oil for frying

Pea hummus:

300 g (10½ oz) cooked peas
100 g (3½ oz/⅔ cup) cooked chickpeas
100 ml (3½ fl oz/scant ½ cup) olive oil
1 tbsp tahini
1 garlic clove, peeled
freshly squeezed juice of ½ lemon
3 tbsp finely chopped fresh mint
sea salt

To serve:

6 burger buns
butter for the buns
pea shoots
zest of 1 lemon

Instructions:

1. Preheat the oven to 200°C (400°F/Gas 6).
2. Scrub and trim the beetroots. Dry them completely and brush them with oil. Put a layer of coarse sea salt at the bottom of an ovenproof dish and place the beetroots on this bed of salt, leaving small spaces between them. Sprinkle sea salt over the beetroots so it almost covers them, and poke the cloves of garlic and the oregano in between them (see photo on the next page).
3. Bake the beetroots in the oven until they are soft, for about 40 minutes. When they look a little shrivelled and grey on the outside they will usually be perfect inside. Take them out and let them cool.
4. Make the pepper seasoning as described on page 132.
5. Cut the beetroots into small matchsticks, or grate them with a mandoline or grater.
6. Put the 1 teaspoon of roasted pepper seasoning, rice, panko breadcrumbs and almond butter into a food processor and mix to create a fairly smooth consistency. Transfer to a bowl and add the beetroot matchsticks, lentils and quinoa. Add a little salt to taste as necessary.
7. Take a handful of mixture at a time and shape into 6 round patties, either by hand or using a food ring (see page 10). Put the patties on a plate and cover with cling film (plastic wrap). Put in the fridge for at least an hour, preferably longer, so they hold their shape when frying.
8. Preheat the oven to 180°C (350°F/Gas 4).
9. Mix all the ingredients for the pea hummus in a food processor or using a hand blender until the mixture has a smooth consistency. If you want your hummus to be a little more chunky, you can you chuck in the peas at the end and pulse-blend the mixture a few times.
10. Heat a few tablespoons of oil in a frying pan (skillet). Fry the patties over a medium heat for a few minutes on both sides until they develop a nice surface. Transfer them to an ovenproof dish and bake for 5–10 minutes.
11. Butter the buns on the cut surface and fry them quickly in a frying pan or grill (broil) them in the oven.
12. Place a patty on the bottom of each bun. Ladle over a little pea hummus and top with pea shoots and lemon zest.

#29

SALT-ROASTED BEETROOT BURGER WITH PICKLED REDCURRANTS AND SPINACH

- -

For 6 burgers:

800 g (1 lb 12 oz) beetroots (beets)
2–3 tbsp olive or rapeseed oil
coarse sea salt
6–7 garlic cloves, peeled
fresh thyme and oregano

Mushroom jus:
1 tsp Roasted Pepper Seasoning (see page 132)
1-2 tablespoons dried mushrooms, preferably shiitake or porcini
1 red onion
1–2 tbsp sherry
1 tsp honey

Quick-pickled redcurrants:
1 tbsp white wine vinegar
1 tsp sugar
2 tbsp redcurrants

To serve:
6 burger buns
butter for the buns
a few handfuls of fresh spinach
fresh herbs

Instructions:
1. Preheat the oven to 200°C (400°F/Gas 6).
2. Trim and scrub the beetroots. Completely dry them and brush them with oil. Put a layer of coarse sea salt at the bottom of an ovenproof dish and place the beetroots on this bed of salt, leaving small spaces between them. Sprinkle sea salt over the beetroots so it almost covers them, and poke the cloves of garlic and fresh herbs in between them (see photo on previous page).
3. Bake the beetroots in the middle of the oven until they are soft, for about 40 minutes. When they look a little shrivelled and grey on the outside they will should be perfect inside.

4. Make the roasted pepper seasoning as described on page 132.
5. Put the dried mushrooms into a bowl and pour water over them until they are submerged. Cover with a lid or plate and leave for 20 minutes. Strain the liquid off into a saucepan.
6. Peel and halve the onions. Flash-fry them in a dry frying pan (skillet) with the cut surface facing downwards until they are almost completely black. Add the 1 teaspoon of roasted pepper seasoning, onion and sherry to the saucepan of mushroom juice. Bring to the boil and considerably reduce, until it has a thick, syrup-like consistency. Strain off the liquid, add the honey and stir together to make a thick jus.
7. Peel the beetroots and cut them into small cubes (I usually use rubber gloves to avoid staining my hands).
8. For the quick-pickled redcurrants, heat the vinegar and sugar in a small saucepan. Stir until the sugar has dissolved. Add the redcurrants and remove the saucepan from the heat. Put to one side.
9. Put the beetroot cubes into the saucepan of mushroom jus. Cook over a low heat, stirring carefully now and again so that everything combines well. The reduced mushroom jus acts as a sort of glue and will help the patties hold together better.
10. Lift out the beetroot cubes with a slotted spoon and press them down into a food ring (see page 10) or shape them with your hands to form 6 round patties.
11. Butter the buns on the cut surface and fry them quickly in a frying pan or grill them in the oven.
12. Put a little spinach at the bottom of each bun, top with a beetroot patty and finish with pickled redcurrants and some fresh herbs.

#30

BLACKENED RACLETTE BURGER
WITH PICKLED BABY ONIONS,
PARSLEY AND LEMON OIL

For 6 burgers:

1 lemon
100 ml (3½ fl oz/scant ½ cup) olive oil
600 g (1 lb 5 oz) raclette

Quick-pickled baby onions:

12 baby onions
salt
100 ml (3½ fl oz/scant ½ cup) malt or red wine vinegar
100 g (3½ oz/scant ½ cup) cane sugar
100 ml (3½ fl oz/scant ½ cup) water
1 tbsp mustard seeds
2 tsp whole black peppercorns
2 tsp coriander seeds

To serve:

6 burger buns
butter for the buns
fresh parsley
2 finely chopped garlic cloves

Instructions:

1. Peel the baby onions and cut a cross in the top of each of them. Bring some salted water (approx. 1 tablespoon of salt to 1.5 litres/50 fl oz/6 cups of water) to the boil and add the onions. Boil them for 8–10 minutes. Drain the onions and rinse them until they are cold. Put to one side. Bring the vinegar, sugar, water, mustard seeds, black peppercorns and coriander seeds to the boil and stir for about 2 minutes, until the sugar has dissolved. Put the onions into a sterilised jar and pour the hot liquor over them. Allow to cool, then put the lid on. Leave in the fridge for at least an hour.

2. Wash the lemon. Shave the peel from half of the lemon with a vegetable peeler and finely grate the other half. Put the lemon-peel shavings into a small saucepan (save the zest for later).

3. Add the olive oil to the lemon peel in the saucepan and heat over a medium heat. Take the saucepan from the hob when it starts to simmer and leave it for about 10 minutes so that the oil takes on the flavour of the lemon peel.

4. Slice the cheese into 6 pieces. Heat a dry frying pan (skillet) over a very high heat. Put the cheese slices in when the pan is really hot, and quickly fry the cheese on both sides so it gets a blackened surface. If you have access to a blowtorch you can also blast the cheese towards the end to brown it.

5. Butter the buns on the cut surface and fry them quickly in a frying pan or grill (broil) them in the oven.

6. Put a piece of cheese on each bun and top with pickled baby onions, parsley and a little finely chopped garlic. Finish by drizzling some lemon oil over it and sprinkling a little lemon zest on top.

#31

PANKO-CRUSTED DEEP-FRIED PEA BURGER WITH DEEP-FRIED SEAWEED AND SEA BUCKTHORN MAYONNAISE

For 6 burgers:

200 g (7 oz) Oven-Baked Onions (see page 132)
2 tbsp finely chopped fresh mint
1 tbsp finely chopped fresh lovage
2–3 eggs
50 g (2 oz/scant 1 cup) panko breadcrumbs
800 g (1 lb 12 oz) peas (cooked and cooled
    or thawed frozen ones)
4 garlic cloves
4 spring onions (scallions)

Breading and deep-frying:

3 eggs
90–120 g (3¼–4 oz/approx. ⅔ cup) plain (all-purpose) flour
75 g (2½ oz/1¼ cups) panko breadcrumbs
1 litre (34 fl oz/4 cups) peanut oil
sea salt

Deep-fried seaweed:

120 g (4 oz) dried sea kelp
peanut oil for deep-frying (reuse the oil used for the patties)

To serve:

6 burger buns
butter for the buns
pea shoots
Sea Buckthorn Mayonnaise (see page 126)

Instructions:

1. Bake the onions to the recipe on page 132.
2. Put the oven-baked onions, mint and lovage into a food processor and mix until everything is finely distributed. Add the eggs and panko breadcrumbs and continue mixing so that everything combines well. Finally add the peas and pulse-blend or mix quickly for a few seconds – the peas must just be broken up.

3. Peel the garlic. Finely chop the garlic and spring onions and stir into the mixture.
4. Take a handful of mixture at a time and shape into 6 round patties, either by hand or using a food ring (see page 10). Put the patties on a plate lined with baking parchment. Cover with cling film (plastic wrap) and put in the freezer for a few hours, until completely frozen.
5. Break the eggs for the breading into a bowl and lightly whisk them. Pour the flour and panko breadcrumbs into separate bowls and place them in a row.
6. Preheat the oven to 180°C (350°F/Gas 4).
7. Take the pea patties out of the freezer and dip them first in the flour, then in the beaten egg and finally in the panko breadcrumbs.
8. Fill a high-sided saucepan with the oil and heat to 190°C (375°F), then reduce the heat to medium and try to keep the oil at 190°C (375°F) as far as possible.
9. Deep-fry 2 patties at a time in the oil for 2–3 minutes on both sides, so they develop a nice golden-brown colour, pushing them around with a slotted spoon. Lift them out with the slotted spoon and drain on paper towels (save the deep-frying oil for the seaweed). Sprinkle with salt on both sides. Transfer the patties to an ovenproof dish and bake them in the oven for 5–10 minutes.
10. Heat the oil to 190°C (375°F) again and deep-fry the seaweed. When it has swollen a little and starts to crisp it is ready. Remove using a slotted spoon and drain on a cooling rack with baking parchment underneath.
11. Butter the buns on the cut surface and fry them quickly in a frying pan (skillet) or grill (broil) them in the oven.
12. Place a patty on the bottom of each bun. Put a little deep-fried seaweed and some pea shoots on top. Top off with a generous dollop of sea buckthorn mayonnaise.

burger buns

In this chapter you will find my best recipes for burger buns. Two tips apply to all the bun recipes: 1) Remember that you won't always need to use all the flour – different sorts of flour absorb different amounts of liquid, so it is better to start with a small amount of flour and then add more. 2) The method of shaping the buns is unbeatable. Just google 'dough rounding' and you will find good instructional videos.

SWEET POTATO BUNS

For 10–12 buns:

50 g (2 oz/¼ cup) butter

250 ml (8½ fl oz/1 cup) whole (full-fat) milk

15–20 g (½–1 oz) fresh yeast

2 tbsp sugar

1 tsp salt

1 egg

200 g (7 oz) boiled or salt-roasted sweet potatoes
(see steps 4–5 on page 37)

650 g (1 lb 7 oz/4⅓ cups) plain (all-purpose) flour

1 egg + 1 tbsp water for brushing

sesame seeds

Instructions:

1. Melt the butter over a low heat, then add the milk. Heat to body temperature – approx. 37°C (99°F). Crumble the yeast into a bowl. Pour the milk into the bowl and stir so that the yeast dissolves. Whisk in the sugar, salt and egg.

2. Mash the sweet potatoes with a fork and stir the mash into the contents of the bowl.

3. Mix in the flour a little at a time. Knead the dough for about 5 minutes in a dough mixer or for 10 minutes by hand. It should be elastic and easy to work, and should come away from the edges.

4. Cover the dough with a tea (dish) towel. Leave in a warm place to rise for about 1½–2 hours, or until it has doubled in size.

5. Divide the dough into 10–12 pieces and shape into round balls by folding the edges in towards the middle, so you achieve good surface tension – pretty much like taking an opened flower and folding the petals together to form a bud again. Put the buns on a baking tray lined with baking parchment, with the seam facing downwards, and gently press them with the palm of your hand. Cover with a tea towel and allow them to rise for a further 45 minutes.

6. Preheat the oven to 200°C (400°F/Gas 6).

7. Whisk the egg with 1 tablespoon of water. Brush the tops of the buns with the beaten egg and sprinkle a few sesame seeds over them.

8. Put the buns in the oven and reduce the heat to 180°C (350°F/Gas 4). Bake for 10–15 minutes, depending on size. Take a bun out after 10 minutes and tap the bottom – if it sounds hollow it is done. Allow to cool on a cooling rack and store them in a ziplock bag.

In this recipe I use sweet potatoes, but you can of course replace them with ordinary potatoes, or you might try out another root vegetable such as parsnips or Jerusalem artichokes.

#02

CHARCOAL BUNS

- -

For 10–12 buns:

Ingredients for Sweet Potato Buns (see page 97)
15 g (½ oz) active charcoal powder (see page 156)

Instructions:
Follow the recipe for the sweet potato buns, but add the charcoal powder when you add the milk. Thoroughly stir in the charcoal powder.

You can find active charcoal in health food shops and on the internet. Apart from giving you the most amazing jet-black buns, charcoal is said to be good for your health.

03

POOLISH-BASED BURGER BUNS

For approx. 20 buns:

approx. 1–2 teaspoons yeast
500 ml (17 fl oz/2 cups) cold water
750 g (1 lb 2 oz/5 cups) plain (all-purpose) flour
¾–1 tbsp salt
1 egg + 1 tbsp water for brushing
sesame seeds to coat

Instructions:

1. Dissolve the small piece of yeast in the water in a large bowl (the contents will later double in volume). Stir in 500 g (1 lb 2 oz/3⅓ cups) flour and whisk to form an even mixture. Cover with a lid or cling film (plastic wrap) and leave for 12–16 hours at room temperature. The room temperature will affect the fermentation speed, so keep your eye on the poolish (starter) during the final few hours. If you notice that the bubbles in the poolish are getting smaller, then the strength of the yeast is decreasing, in which case you should quickly proceed to the next step.

2. Pour the salt and the remaining flour into the poolish. Knead the dough in a food processor at medium speed for 8 minutes. Let it rest for 10 minutes, then work it for a further 2 minutes. As you have kick-started the fermentation process with the poolish you do not actually need any interim fermentation. But if you want you can let the dough rest for 15 minutes – the gluten in the flour can then develop further and the dough will become more elastic and easier to work.

3. Turn the dough out onto a floured surface. Cut it into 65 g (2¼ oz) chunks using a dough scraper (pulling the dough apart with your hands damages the gluten network). Fold the edges in towards the middle so you achieve good surface tension – pretty much like taking an opened flower and folding the petals together to form a bud again.

4. Distribute the buns, with the seam facing downwards, on two baking trays lined with baking parchment, making sure there is plenty of space between them. Sprinkle a little flour over them, cover them with a tea (dish) towel and let them rise for about 1 hour.

5. Preheat the oven to 250°C (475°F/Gas 9). The buns must be baked at a slightly lower temperature, but as the cold baking tray will lower the oven temperature it is a good idea to have a 'buffer'.

6. Whisk the egg and water. Brush the tops of the buns with the whisked egg and sprinkle over some sesame seeds.

7. Put the baking tray in the middle of the oven, reduce the heat to 230°C (450°F/Gas 8) and bake the buns for about 15 minutes.

8. Take the baking tray out and allow to cool. An important part of the process is allowing the steam in the buns to play its part – the insides will be best if you allow the buns to rest for 30 minutes.

I drew the inspiration for this recipe from Sébastien Boudet's book *The French Baker*. It includes a recipe for fantastic baguettes based on poolish (a starter) – and you can use the same method to make phenomenally good burger buns.

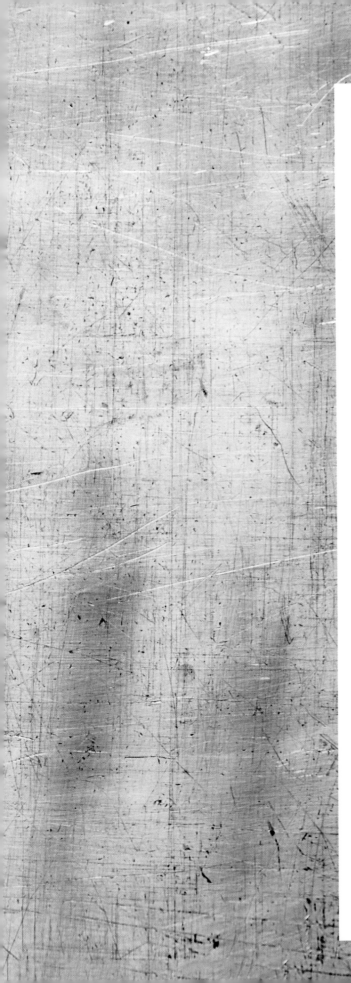

04

BRIOCHE BUNS

- -

For 12–16 buns:

200 ml (7 fl oz/scant 1 cup) whole (full-fat) milk
25 g (1 oz) yeast
4 eggs
1 tbsp caster (superfine) sugar
1 tsp salt
650 g (1 lb 7 oz/4⅓ cups) plain (all-purpose) flour
250 g (9 oz/1 cup) butter at room temperature
1 egg yolk + 1 tbsp single (light) cream for brushing
sesame seeds

Instructions:

1. Heat the milk to body temperature – about 37°C (99°F).
Crumble the yeast into a bowl and whisk in the milk so the
yeast dissolves. Add the eggs, sugar and salt and whisk to
form a smooth mixture.

2. Mix in the flour a little at a time, and knead for 7 minutes
in a dough mixer to make an elastic dough – it must come
away from the edges. The amount of flour can vary, so it is
a good idea to have a little extra to hand.

3. Cut the butter into small chunks and work it into the
dough by kneading for a further 5 minutes in the dough
mixer, until the dough is nice and smooth.

4. Cover the dough with a tea (dish) towel. Leave to rise for
1–1½ hours or until the dough has doubled in size.

5. Divide the dough into 10–12 pieces and shape into
round balls by folding the edges in towards the middle
so you achieve good surface tension – pretty much like
taking an opened flower and folding the petals together to
form a bud again. Put the buns on a baking tray lined with
baking parchment with the seam facing downwards, and
gently press them with the palm of your hand. Cover with a
tea towel and let them rise for a further 1–1½ hours.

6. Fill an ovenproof dish with water and place it right on the
bottom of the oven.

7. Preheat the oven to 225°C (430°F/Gas 7).

8. Whisk the yolk and cream. Brush the tops of the buns
with the beaten egg and sprinkle sesame seeds over.

9. Put the baking tray into the oven and reduce the heat to
200°C (400°F/Gas 6). Bake the buns for 10–15 minutes,
until they have developed some colour. Take a bun out
and tap the bottom of it – if it sounds hollow, it is done.
Otherwise, bake for a further 5 minutes. Take out and allow
to cool on a cooling rack. Store in sealed ziplock bags.

side orders

Side orders by no means play a subsidiary role —
they can equally stand alone! In this chapter you
will find coleslaws, barbecued corn on the cob and
deep-fried favourites.

01

DEEP-FRIED POTATO SHOESTRINGS WITH GRATED TRUFFLE AND TRUFFLE MAYONNAISE

- -

Serves 6

6 large baking potatoes
1 litre (34 fl oz/4 cups) peanut or deep-frying oil
fresh rosemary
sea salt

To serve:
30 g (1 oz) black truffle or a few drops of black truffle oil
200 g (7 oz/scant 1 cup) Truffle Mayonnaise (see page 128)

Instructions:
1. Peel the potatoes, then finely shred them, ideally using a mandoline with a grating attachment.
2. Line a large bowl with a few layers of paper towel.
3. Pour the oil into a high-sided saucepan and heat it to 180°C (355°F), then reduce the heat and try to keep the temperature at 180°C (355°F) as far as possible.
4. Deep-fry the potato shoestrings in the oil for 2–3 minutes, until they are golden brown, turning them with a slotted spoon now and again. Throw the rosemary sprigs into the saucepan towards the end of the deep-frying time.
5. Take the shoestrings out using a slotted spoon and put them in the paper towel-lined bowl so the excess fat is absorbed. Sprinkle them with sea salt and turn them over.
6. Arrange the potato shoestrings on a plate and grate some truffle over them or drizzle over a few drops of truffle oil. Serve with the truffle mayonnaise.

02

DEEP-FRIED SWEET POTATO CRISPS

- -

Serves 6

4 large sweet potatoes
1 litre (34 fl oz/4 cups) peanut or deep-frying oil
sea salt

Instructions:
1. Cut the sweet potatoes into slices as thin as possible, ideally using a mandoline (you do not need to peel the potatoes).
2. Line a large bowl with a few layers of paper towel. Pour the oil into a high-sided saucepan and heat it to 180°C (355°F), then reduce the heat and try to keep the temperature at 180°C (355°F) as far as possible.
3. Deep-fry the sweet potato slices in the oil for 2–3 minutes, or until they are golden brown, turning them now and again using a slotted spoon.
4. Remove the sweet potato crisps (chips) and lay them in the paper towel-lined bowl so the excess fat is absorbed. Sprinkle them with sea salt and turn them so that the salt is evenly distributed.
5. Serve as a snack or an accompaniment, or use them as a burger topping for extra crispiness.

03

DOUBLE-DEEP-FRIED CHIPS DUNKED IN CHEESE AND FRESH HERBS

- -

Serves 6

800 g (1 lb 12 oz) firm potatoes (4-5 medium potatoes)
1 tbsp pickling vinegar
1 tbsp coarse sea salt
1–2 litres (34–68 fl oz/4–8 cups) peanut or deep-frying oil
chopped fresh herbs, e.g. rosemary, thyme and parsley
50–75 g (2–2½ oz/½–⅔ cup) coarsely grated Västerbotten or
    other strong hard cheese

To serve:
Tomato Ketchup (see page 131)

Day 1:
1. Cut the potatoes into 1 cm- (½ in-) thick sticks (you do not need to peel them first).
2. Put the potatoes in a saucepan containing plenty of water – about 2 litres (68 fl oz/8 cups) – and add the vinegar and salt. Bring to the boil, then boil for 5–10 minutes. Make sure the potatoes do not go *too* soft and fall apart – the cooking time can vary from one type of potato to another. Drain the potatoes and transfer them to a tea (dish) towel.
3. Pour the oil into a high-sided saucepan and heat to 200°C (390°F). Reduce the heat to medium and try to keep the temperature at 200°C (390°F) as far as possible.
4. Deep-fry a third of the potato sticks at a time, for about 1 minute, whilst pushing them round with a slotted spoon.
5. Lift the chips (fries) out with a slotted spoon, transfer to a metal colander and drain. Cool, cover with cling film (plastic wrap) and freeze overnight. (Save the oil for the next day.)

Day 2:
1. Line a bowl with a few layers of paper towel.
2. In a high-sided saucepan, heat the oil from the day before to 200°C (390°F). Reduce the heat to medium and try to keep the temperature at 200°C (390°F) as far as possible.
3. Deep-fry the chips a third at a time for 3–4 minutes, or until they are golden, turning them around with a slotted spoon now and again. Put them on the paper towel-lined bowl so excess oil is absorbed. Sprinkle with sea salt and turn them over.
4. Remove the paper towel and sprinkle the herbs and cheese over the chips. Mix well and serve straight away.

Wash the potatoes before peeling them (but do not scrub them so hard that the peel completely disappears). Save the peel and try deep-frying it – the thinner the peel, the better the flavour! See the recipe on page 111.

04

ROASTED SWEET POTATO CHIPS
WITH GRATED SWISS CHEESE

- -

Serves 6

4 large sweet potatoes
3 tbsp peanut oil
sea salt
2 garlic cloves
3 tbsp butter
2 tbsp finely chopped fresh parsley
50 g (2 oz) Belper Knolle (Swiss hard cheese)
   or Parmesan

Instructions:
1. Preheat the oven to 200°C (400°F/Gas 6).
2. Cut the sweet potatoes into sticks 5 mm (¼ in) thick (you do not need to peel them first). Spread the sweet potatoes out on a baking tray lined with baking parchment. Drizzle over the oil and sprinkle with salt. Roast the sweet potatoes for 20–30 minutes. Stir now and then.
3. Peel the cloves of garlic and crush them using the thick edge of a knife. Put the garlic into a cold saucepan together with the butter. Melt the butter over a low heat. Put the saucepan to one side and leave for a few minutes so the butter takes on the flavour of the garlic. Pour the melted butter into a bowl (throw away the scrapings and the garlic).
4. Put the chips (fries) on a plate, spoon over the melted butter and sprinkle the parsley on top. Grate the cheese over them and serve.

05

DOUBLE-DEEP-FRIED POTATO
PEEL WITH GARLIC MAYONNAISE

- -

Serves 6

1 litre (34 fl oz/4 cups) peanut or deep-frying oil
600 g (1 lb 5 oz) potato peelings
sea salt

To serve:
200 g (7 oz/scant 1 cup) Garlic Mayonnaise (see page 128)

Instructions:
1. Place the oil in a high-sided saucepan and heat to 160°C (320°F), then reduce the heat to medium and try to keep the temperature at 160°C (320°F) as far as possible.
2. Put the potato peelings in the oil and leave for about 5 minutes, or until they are soft. Take them out using a slotted spoon, transfer to a colander and drain.
3. Line a large bowl with a few layers of paper towel and put it next to the cooker. Heat up the oil again, to 180°C (355°F). Reduce the heat to medium and try to keep the temperature at 180°C (355°F) as far as possible.
4. Deep-fry the potato peelings until they are golden brown, about 2–3 minutes. (See photo on the next page.) Turn them using a slotted spoon now and again.
5. Lift the peelings out with the slotted spoon and transfer them to the paper towel-lined bowl so excess fat is absorbed. Sprinkle with sea salt and turn them so the salt is evenly distributed. Serve with garlic mayonnaise.

```
Belper Knolle is a small hard cheese
that looks a bit like a truffle. It comes
from the village of Belp, near Bern in
Switzerland, and was developed by the
cheese producer Herr Glauser. The cheese
is made from raw cow's milk, and is then
rolled in a herb mix comprising Himalayan
salt, locally grown garlic and pepper
from the Bernese Oberland region. It is
excellent grated over chips!
```

My two best deep-frying tips: Use a good-quality enamelled stock pot. I have tried deep-frying in all possible types of stock pots and saucepans, but the results have never really been as good. Not only do enamelled stock pots have a thick base, but the enamel surfaces insulate and contribute towards holding the heat. I have also discovered that peanut oil is superior for deep-frying; it stays very hot, has a neutral flavour and can be reused more often than all the other oils I have tested.

06

DEEP-FRIED COURGETTE FLOWERS STUFFED WITH CREAM CHEESE AND PARMESAN

- -

Serves 6

12 courgette (zucchini) flowers
120 g (4 oz/generous ¾ cup) plain (all-purpose) flour
1 tsp baking powder
½ tsp sea salt
1 egg
200 ml (7 fl oz/scant 1 cup) beer, such as lager or brown ale
1 litre (34 fl oz/4 cups) peanut or deep-frying oil
sea salt

Filling:
120 g (4 oz/½ cup) cream cheese
2 tbsp single (light) cream
2 tbsp grated Parmesan
sea salt and freshly ground black pepper

Instructions:
1. Rinse the courgette flowers in cold water to get rid of all the dirt. Leave them on a tea (dish) towel to dry.
2. Mix the flour, baking powder and salt in a bowl. Whisk the egg in another bowl, then stir the whisked egg and beer into the flour mixture. Stir to form an even mixture.
3. Mix the cream cheese, cream and Parmesan in a bowl. Season to taste. Put the cream cheese filling into a piping bag and pipe a little filling into each flower. Carefully fold the flower petals in so the filling does not run out.
4. Line a bowl with a few layers of paper towel and put it next to the cooker.
5. Heat plenty of oil to 180°C (355°F) in a high-sided saucepan. Reduce the heat and try to keep the temperature at 180°C (355°F) as far as possible.
6. Dip the flowers in the deep-frying mixture and deep-fry 3–4 flowers at a time for about 2 minutes, or until they are golden brown. Push them around carefully with a slotted spoon now and again.
7. Lift the courgette flowers out and drain on the paper towel-lined bowl. Sprinkle with salt and turn them so the salt is evenly distributed. Serve straight away.

07

BARBECUED CORN ON THE COB WITH GARLIC BUTTER, CRÈME FRAÎCHE AND PARMESAN

- -

Serves 6

6 corn cobs with husks
2 garlic cloves
150 g (5 oz/generous ½ cup) butter at room temperature
3 lemons
200 g (7 oz/generous ¾ cup) crème fraîche
3 thinly sliced jalapeños
sea salt
100 g (3½ oz/1 cup) grated Parmesan

Instructions:
1. Bring a large pan of lightly salted water to the boil.
2. Fold over the husks of the corn on the cob and remove the silk that lies between the husks and the kernels. Put the corn into the boiling water with the tips pointing downwards and boil for about 5 minutes. Take them out and fold the husks back again.
3. Light the barbecue. Barbecue the corn well all over while the barbecue is still actively flaming. If you want you can put the corn on the cob straight onto the burning charcoal – just make sure you use charcoal that has not been chemically treated. Barbecue the corn until the husks are almost completely black (they act as a protective casing around the corn kernels).
4. Take the corn on the cob from the barbecue and put to one side.
5. Peel and finely chop the garlic. Mix the butter and garlic with a fork in a bowl.
6. Rinse, dry and halve the lemons, and barbecue them with the cut surface facing downwards until they have developed a nice colour.
7. Remove the husks and put the corn onto a plate. Spread with garlic butter, drizzle over a little crème fraîche and sprinkle some sliced jalapeño on top. Add salt and grate Parmesan over them. Serve the corn on the cob together with the grilled lemon halves.

08

FENNEL, CARROT AND SAVOY CABBAGE COLESLAW

Serves 10

2–3 carrots (approx. 200 g/7 oz)
500 g (1 lb 2 oz) savoy cabbage
300 g (10½ oz) fennel
zest of 1 lemon + 2 tbsp freshly squeezed lemon juice
2 tbsp finely chopped fresh lovage or parsley
1 tbsp Pickled Mustard Seeds (see page 136)
lemon segments to serve

Coleslaw dressing:

2 tsp fennel seeds
1 tsp dill seeds
1 tsp whole black peppercorns
200 g (7 oz/generous ¾ cup) mayonnaise
2–3 tbsp apple cider vinegar
½ tsp sea salt

Instructions:

1. For the coleslaw dressing, roast the fennel seeds, dill seeds and whole black peppercorns in a dry cast-iron pan over a medium heat until the seeds are golden brown. Pound the spices in a mortar or grind them to a fine powder in a spice mixer.

2. Put the spice mix in a bowl and pour in the rest of the ingredients for the coleslaw dressing. Whisk until fluffy.

3. Peel the carrots and trim the cabbage and fennel. Thinly slice the carrots, savoy cabbage and fennel, ideally using a mandoline. Transfer them to a bowl and pour the lemon juice over them. Knead well with your hands.

4. Stir in the dressing and top with the lemon zest, lovage or parsley and the pickled mustard seeds. Serve with the lemon segments.

KOHLRABI AND SWEETHEART CABBAGE COLESLAW

Serves 10

1 batch of coleslaw dressing (see recipe on the left)
400 g (14 oz) kohlrabi
500 g (1 lb 2 oz) sweetheart (hipsi) cabbage
2–3 spring onions (scallions)
50 g (2 oz) fresh horseradish
zest of 1 lemon + 2 tbsp freshly squeezed lemon juice
finely chopped fresh dill
2 tbsp olive oil

Instructions:

1. Make the dressing as described on the left.

2. Peel the kohlrabi and remove the coarse part of the cabbage and kohlrabi roots. Thinly slice the spring onions, kohlrabi and cabbage, ideally using a mandoline, then transfer the slices to a bowl.

3. Peel and finely grate the horseradish. Put the horseradish in the bowl with the cabbage and fennel. Mix in the lemon juice and knead well with your hands.

4. Fold in the dressing and top with the dill and lemon zest. Finish by drizzling some olive oil on top.

PURPLE SWEETHEART CABBAGE AND APPLE SAUERKRAUT

- -

Serves 6

500 g (1 lb 2 oz) purple sweetheart (hipsi) cabbage
1 ½ tsp iodine-free salt
1 apple (approx. 150 g/5 oz)
1 tsp fennel seeds

Instructions:

1. Shred the cabbage as thinly as possible, ideally using a mandoline. Put it into a bowl, sprinkle the salt over it and knead well. Put to one side.

2. Rinse the apple and remove the core (keep the peel). Shred the apple finely, either with a mandoline or using an ordinary grater.

3. Add the apple shreds and fennel seeds to the bowl of cabbage and knead well for about 10 minutes so liquid is released from the cabbage.

4. Sterilise a 1 litre- (34 fl oz-) jar (preferably one with a rubber sealing ring and metal clip such as a Kilner or Mason jar). Put the cabbage mixture into a jar a little at a time. Press down with a wooden spoon so it all fits in. Finish by pouring over the liquid from the cabbage. Put the lid on and seal using the metal clip.

5. Put the jar in a plastic bag (leaving the bag open) and put it on a plate. In all likelihood quite a bit of liquid will escape through the rubber seal – hence the protective bag around it.

6. Leave the jar at room temperature for 14 days, then put it in the fridge and leave for at least 2 weeks to allow the flavours to develop properly. Serve as an accompaniment or a burger topping (see, for example, the Deep-Fried Mushroom and Quinoa Burger on page 17).

pickles, condiments and other accompaniments

I am a bit obsessed with pickles, kimchi, spreads and mixes and other tasty accompaniments. They are often at least as important as the actual burger, and several of the recipes in this chapter play a prominent role in the burgers in this book. Pickles taste a lot better if you do your own pickling instead of buying them ready-made.

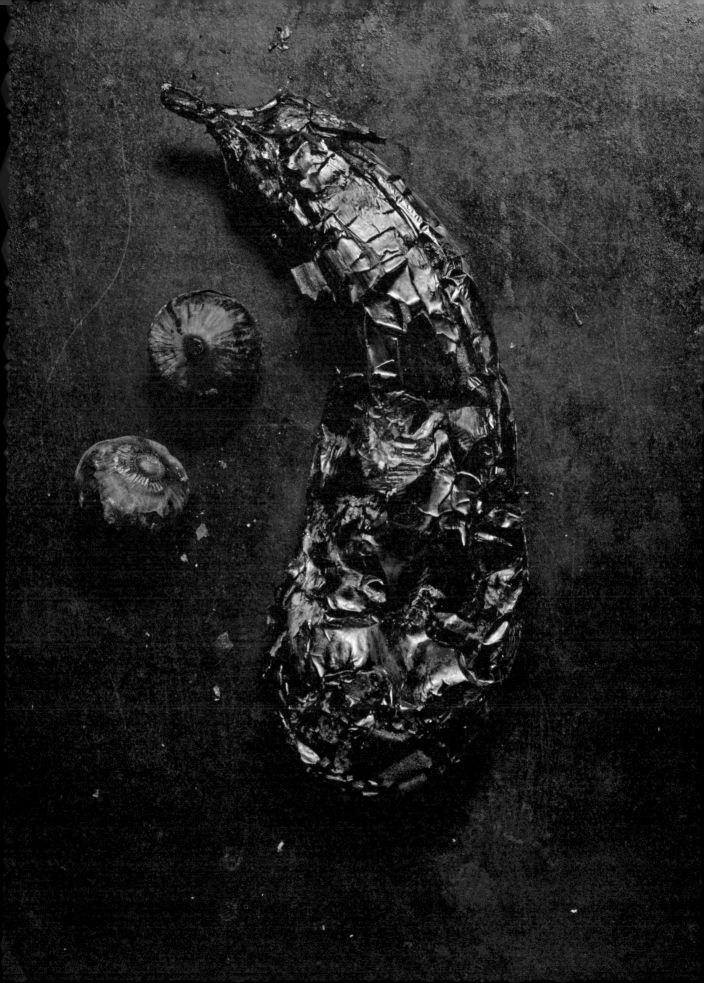

01

CHARCOAL-ROASTED BABA GHANOUSH

- -

Makes about 1 litre (34 fl oz/4 cups) and 6 as a side

3 medium aubergines (eggplants)
3 garlic cloves
zest and freshly squeezed juice of 1 lemon
100 ml (3½ fl oz/scant ½ cup) olive oil + a little extra to serve
sea salt and freshly ground black pepper
1 tsp mild chilli powder, e.g. piment d'Espelette

Instructions:
1. Light the barbecue.
2. Prick a few holes in the aubergines with a toothpick, then put them straight onto the glowing charcoal. You can also do this when the charcoal is actively flaming. Make sure you use charcoal that has not been chemically treated. Cook the aubergines until the skins are completely charred and they are soft inside. This takes about 15 minutes. Put on the garlic cloves (with skins) for the final 5–10 minutes and roast until they are also soft inside.
3. Let the garlics and aubergines cool a little, so you can handle them, then cut them in half lengthways and scoop out the flesh with a spoon (try to get as much of the flesh out as possible). Split the garlic cloves and scoop out the insides.
4. Put the garlic and the aubergine flesh into a large bowl. Pour in the lemon juice and a little of the oil, then beat with a whisk. Pour in the rest of the oil a little at a time, stirring vigorously. If you want a firmer consistency you can use less oil. Add salt and pepper to taste.
5. Put the aubergine mix into a bowl. Dust it with the chilli powder, sprinkle over the lemon zest and drizzle a little olive oil on top. Serve as an accompaniment on the side or spread the mix straight onto the burger. You can also use it as part of the actual patty (see the Baba Ghanoush and Borlotti Burger on page 26), but if doing so remember to use less oil, otherwise the patty will be not be firm enough.

Try to get out as much as possible of the brown aubergine flesh right next to the charred skin. That is where the tasty, smoky flavour of the charcoal-grilled aubergine comes from.

- -

02

BASIC MAYONNAISE RECIPE

- -

Makes about 650 ml (21 fl oz/2½ cups)

2 eggs
1 tbsp Dijon mustard
1 tbsp white wine vinegar
2 tbsp cold-pressed olive oil
500 ml (17 fl oz/2 cups) rapeseed oil (not cold-pressed)
sea salt and freshly ground black pepper

Instructions:
1. Break the eggs into a jug or a tall, narrow bowl. Add the Dijon mustard, vinegar and olive oil, for extra flavour. If you only use cold-pressed olive oil in the mayonnaise it will be a little too bitter – but a splash of it makes for a great flavour, especially if the mayonnaise is otherwise plain.
2. Mix with a stick blender until everything is well combined. Then position the stick blender at the bottom of the bowl and add the rapeseed oil in a thin stream whilst mixing (keeping the blender at the bottom of the bowl). When you notice that the mayonnaise is starting to set, draw the blender upwards. Continue to mix until you have a good consistency, and add salt and pepper to taste.
3. Store the mayonnaise in a jar or bottle in the fridge. Keeps for several weeks.

03

SEA BUCKTHORN MAYONNAISE

- -

Makes 500 ml (17 fl oz/2 cups)

300 g (10½ oz) Basic Mayonnaise (see recipe on the left)
75 g (3 oz/scant ½ cup) sea buckthorn berries
1 tsp coriander seeds
1 tbsp apple cider vinegar
2 tbsp olive oil

Instructions:
1. Make the mayonnaise using the recipe on the left.
2. Mix the sea buckthorn, coriander seeds, apple cider vinegar and oil in a bowl, then press the mix through a fine-mesh sieve to separate off the coriander seed husks and small hard seeds in the sea buckthorn berries.
3. Carefully fold the sea buckthorn into the mayonnaise.

04

CHIPOTLE MAYONNAISE

- -

Makes 500 ml (17 fl oz/2 cups)

300 g (10½ oz) Basic Mayonnaise (see recipe on the left)
4 chipotle chillies in adobo sauce
3 tbsp crème fraîche
freshly squeezed juice of 1 lime

Instructions:
1. Make the mayonnaise using the recipe on the left.
2. Mix the chipotle chillies, crème fraîche and lime juice in a food processor or using a hand blender.
3. Fold the chipotle mixture into the mayonnaise.

For a successful mayonnaise all the ingredients should be at the same temperature.

05

GARLIC MAYONNAISE

- -

Makes 500 ml (17 fl oz/2 cups)

300 g (10½ oz) Basic Mayonnaise (see page 126)
2–3 garlic cloves
1 tbsp freshly squeezed lemon juice
1 tbsp olive oil
1 egg yolk

Instructions:
1. Make the mayonnaise using the recipe on page 126.
2. Peel and finely chop or press the garlic. Put the garlic, lemon juice, oil and egg yolk into a bowl and whisk.
3. Fold the garlic mixture into the mayonnaise and mix together carefully.

06

TRUFFLE MAYONNAISE

- -

Makes 500 ml (17 fl oz/2 cups)

300 g (10½ oz) Basic Mayonnaise (see page 126)
15 g (½ oz) fresh black truffle
3 tbsp crème fraîche

Instructions:
1. Make the mayonnaise using the recipe on page 126.
2. Finely grate the truffle with a grater. Mix the truffle and crème fraîche in a bowl. If you do not have access to fresh truffle you can use a few drops of black truffle oil instead.
3. Carefully stir the truffle cream into the mayonnaise. Ideally, grate a little fresh truffle over it to serve.

07

BLACKENED MAYONNAISE

- -

Makes 500 ml (17 fl oz/2 cups)

300 g (10½ oz) Basic Mayonnaise (see page 126)
  (leave out the white wine vinegar, olive oil and salt)
tops of 3–4 spring onions (scallions)
3 black garlic cloves (see page 156)
2 ancho chillies
2 tbsp sherry vinegar
1 tsp pounded Black Lava salt or ordinary fine salt

Instructions:
1. Make the mayonnaise using the recipe on page 126, but exclude the vinegar, olive oil and salt.
2. Preheat the oven to maximum heat.
3. Cut the spring onion tops lengthways and rinse them clean. Thoroughly dry them.
4. Put them on a baking tray lined with baking parchment and grill (broil) them for a few minutes until they are completely black. Turn the tops over and grill so that the other side is blackened too. Remove them and cool.
5. Put the burnt tops into a bowl and mix to a fine powder with a hand blender.
6. Add the garlic, ancho chillies, vinegar and salt to the mixed tops in the bowl. Mix to an even consistency. Add the mixture to the mayonnaise and mix carefully.

TOMATO KETCHUP

- -

Makes 500 ml (17 fl oz/2 cups)

1 kg (2 lb 3 oz) plum tomatoes
sea salt and freshly ground black pepper
pinch of ground cinnamon
pinch of ground allspice
pinch of ground cloves
1 tsp coriander seeds
2 tsp grated fresh ginger
2 tsp onion powder
2 tsp paprika powder
2 tbsp apple cider vinegar
1 tbsp sherry vinegar
1 tbsp honey
200 ml (7 fl oz/scant 1 cup) water

Instructions:
1. Preheat the oven to 140°C (275°F/Gas 1).
2. Halve the tomatoes and lay them on a baking tray lined with baking parchment, with the cut surfaces uppermost. Sprinkle with salt and pepper, and bake in the middle of the oven for 2 hours.
3. Bring the baked tomatoes and other ingredients to the boil in a heavy-based saucepan. Then reduce the heat and simmer for about 30 minutes.
4. Remove the saucepan from the heat and blend the contents with a hand blender until smooth, then pass the tomato mixture through a fine-mesh sieve (using a spoon to press out as much of the mixture as possible).
5. Wash the saucepan and pour the tomato sauce back into it. Bring the tomato sauce to the boil again and cook for about 30 minutes to reduce to a creamy ketchup. The consistency will get creamier when the ketchup cools, so it is a good idea to test it by putting a spoonful on a plate and allowing it to cool to make sure the consistency is good.
6. Pour the ketchup into clean, sterilised glass bottles. Store in the fridge.

Try flavouring the ketchup with roasted cavolo nero! Finely chop the cavolo nero (see page 147) and fold it into 100 g (3¼ oz) tomato ketchup. Then add another 300 g (10½ oz) ketchup and mix well. You can also make a kimchi-spiced ketchup by mixing one part kimchi stock (see page 140 or 143) and two parts ketchup.

OVEN-BAKED ONIONS

- -

Makes about 500 g (1 lb 2 oz/2 cups)

4 onions (about 600 g/1 lb 5 oz)
2 tbsp butter
olive oil, for drizzling
sea salt and freshly ground black pepper

Instructions:
1. Preheat the oven to 200°C (400°F/Gas 6).
2. Peel the onions and cut them into quarters. Put them in an ovenproof dish, add the butter and drizzle the olive oil over them. Sprinkle with salt and pepper. Bake the onions in the middle of the oven for 20–30 minutes or until they have developed some colour – they can even be a little burnt. Take out and allow to cool.

10

ROASTED PEPPER SEASONING

- -

2 tbsp coriander seeds
2 tbsp Sichuan pepper
2 tbsp whole black peppercorns

Instructions:
1. Heat a dry cast-iron pan over a medium heat. Toast the coriander seeds, Sichuan pepper and black peppercorns until the seeds start to go golden brown and there is a clear spice aroma.
2. Pound the spices in a mortar or mix them to a fine powder with a hand blender. Store in a jar.

GREEN BANANA GUACAMOLE

- -

Serves around 8-10

2 garlic cloves
2 tbsp chopped fresh parsley
2 tbsp chopped fresh coriander (cilantro)
2 tsp cane sugar
zest and freshly squeezed juice of 1 lime
5 unripe green bananas
50 g (2 oz/scant ½ cup) finely chopped pistachios
200 g (7 oz/generous ¾ cup) crème fraîche
2 tbsp finely chopped shallots
sea salt and freshly ground black pepper

Instructions:
1. Peel the garlic. Put the garlic, parsley, coriander, sugar, lime zest and juice in a food processor or blender. Mix to a smooth consistency.
2. Mash the bananas with a fork. Put the mashed bananas, pistachios, crème fraîche, shallots and the herb mix into a bowl. Mix with a fork, and season to taste. Serve as a dip, or slap the mixture straight onto the burgers – see, for example, the Lentil and Charcoal-Roasted Carrot Burger on page 81.

PICKLED MUSTARD SEEDS

- -

Makes about 250 ml (8 fl oz/1 cup)

4 tbsp mustard seeds – ideally a mix of yellow and brown
50 ml (2 fl oz/¼ cup) pickling vinegar
100 g (3½ oz/scant ½ cup) cane sugar
150 ml (5 fl oz/⅔ cup) water

Instructions:
1. Bring the mustard seeds to the boil in a pan of lightly salted water. Reduce the heat and simmer until the seeds are completely soft – this will take 40 minutes–1 hour. Discard the liquid, reserving the mustard seeds.
2. Bring the vinegar, sugar, water and mustard seeds to the boil. Stir until the sugar has dissolved. Remove the saucepan from the heat and allow it to cool.
3. Transfer everything to a sterilised jar and store the pickled seeds in the fridge.

#13

PICKLED RED ONIONS

- -

You need:
4 red onions
100 ml (3½ fl oz/scant ½ cup) pickling vinegar
150 g (5 oz/scant ¾ cup) cane sugar
200 ml (7 fl oz/scant 1 cup) water
1 tsp freshly squeezed lemon juice
1 bay leaf
1 tsp whole black peppercorns
1 tsp Sichuan pepper

Instructions:
1. Peel the onions and cut them into slices 5 mm (¼ in) thick. Put them into a sterilised jar.
2. Bring the other ingredients to the boil to make a solution. Stir until the sugar has dissolved. Strain the solution into the jar of onions. Leave for at least an hour before serving.

#14

PICKLED GHERKINS

- -

Makes about 2 litres (68 fl oz/8 cups)

500 ml (17 fl oz/2 cups) water
6 tbsp salt
1 kg (2 lb 3 oz) gherkins
10 dill heads
2 tbsp Pickled Mustard Seeds (see recipe on the left)

Vinegar solution:
150 ml (5 fl oz/⅔ cup) pickling vinegar
150 g (5 oz/scant ¾ cup) cane sugar
400 ml (13 fl oz/1½ cups) water

Day 1:
1. Mix the 500 ml (17 fl oz/2 cups) water with the salt in a large bowl. Stir until the salt has dissolved. Clean the gherkins with a soft brush and prick a few holes in each of them with a fork or toothpick. Put the gherkins into the salt solution and cover with cling film (plastic wrap). Leave in the fridge for 24 hours.

Day 2:
1. Pour off the salt solution and drain the gherkins in a colander. Cut them into slices 5 mm (¼ in) thick. Then alternate the gherkins, dill heads and mustard seeds in a sterilised jar.
2. Bring all the ingredients for the vinegar solution to the boil and stir until the sugar has dissolved. Remove from the heat and pour the solution straight over the gherkins. Allow to cool, then put the lid on. Store in a cool, dark place. The gherkins will be ready after a week.

- -

#15
PICKLED RADISHES

- -

Makes about 2 litres (68 fl oz/8 cups)

1 kg (2 lb 3 oz) radishes
200 ml (7 fl oz/scant 1 cup) pickling vinegar
400 g (14 oz/scant 2 cups) cane sugar
600 ml (20 fl oz/2½ cups) water
1 tbsp whole black peppercorns
1 tbsp Sichuan pepper
2 tsp coriander seeds

Instructions:
1. Clean the radishes thoroughly, but retain as much of the skin as possible and leave some of the tops in place.
2. Bring the other ingredients to the boil and stir until the sugar has dissolved.
3. Put the radishes in a sterilised jar and pour the hot solution over them. Allow to cool and then put on the lid. Store the jar in a cool, dark place. After a week the pickled radishes will be ready.

PICKLED SEA BUCKTHORN BERRIES

- -

Makes about 500 g (1 lb 2 oz/2 cups)

50–75 g (2 oz–2½ oz) fresh turmeric
50 ml (2 fl oz/¼ cup) pickling vinegar
100 g (3½ oz/scant ½ cup) cane sugar
150 ml (5 fl oz/⅔ cup) water
4 tbsp sea buckthorn berries
2 tonka beans
1 tbsp coriander seeds
1 tsp whole black peppercorns
4 star anise fruits
peel from ¼ Seville orange

Instructions:
1. Halve the turmeric lengthways. Bring the turmeric, vinegar, sugar and water to the boil. Stir until the sugar has dissolved. Take the saucepan from the heat and allow to cool.
2. Put the sea buckthorn berries, tonka beans, coriander seeds, black peppercorns, star anise and Seville orange peel into a sterilised jar and pour the turmeric liquid over them.

KIMCHI BASE

- -

Makes about 500 g (1 lb 2 oz/2 cups)

500 ml (17 fl oz/2 cups) water
2 tbsp rice flour
100 g (3½ oz) miso paste
2 tbsp cane sugar
4 shallots
2 carrots
approx. 12 g (½ oz) fresh ginger
10 finely chopped garlic cloves
65 g (2¼ oz/1¼ cups) chopped fresh coriander (cilantro)
200 g (7 oz/1½ cups) gochugaru (Korean dried chilli)

Instructions:

1. Pour the water and rice flour into a saucepan and bring to the boil. Stir constantly to stop lumps forming. Reduce the heat and add the miso paste and sugar. Simmer for about 5 minutes, stirring now and then. Take the saucepan from the heat and leave to cool. If you want you can leave the mixture in the fridge overnight.

2. Peel the shallots, carrots and ginger and cut them into big chunks. Put the shallots, carrots, ginger, garlic and coriander into a food processor and mix to form a fine purée. If the ingredients are tough to mix you can add a splash of water.

3. Pour the rice flour mixture, vegetable purée and gochugaru into a bowl – preferably stainless steel, as the bright-red kimchi base easily stains. Mix well. The kimchi base keeps well in the fridge. If you are not going to use it for a long time you can also freeze it.

18

COURGETTE KIMCHI

- -

Makes about 700 g (1 lb 9 oz/4½ cups)

1 kg (2 lb 3 oz) courgettes (zucchini)
200 g (7 oz) peeled mooli (daikon)
1¼ tbsp salt
150 g (5 oz/⅔ cup) Kimchi Base (see recipe on the left)

Instructions:

1. Shred the courgettes and the mooli with a mandoline, preferably using a grating attachment, to produce long, thin strips.

2. Put the courgettes and mooli into a bowl. Massage in the salt with your hands and leave at room temperature for at least an hour so the vegetables have time to release their liquid.

3. Add the kimchi base to the bowl of courgettes and mooli. Mix carefully with a wooden spoon.

4. Sterilise a 1 litre- (34 fl oz-) jar (preferably one with a rubber sealing ring and metal clip such as a Kilner or Mason jar). Pack the kimchi into the jar a little at a time. Press it down with a wooden spoon so you get it all in (including the liquid).

5. Seal the jar and put it on a plate – it is a good idea to slip a plastic bag around it, as in all probability a fair bit of liquid will escape (just make sure you do not seal the top of the bag). Leave the jar at room temperature for 3 days. For a more acidic kimchi, leave it at room temperature for up to 5 days. This is something I think you should experiment with over time, to find the flavour you like best.

6. Put the jar in the fridge and leave for at least 1 week so the flavours can develop (I usually leave the kimchi for at least 2 weeks before I use it, but it is a matter of taste). The kimchi will form a spicy liquid, which can be used to flavour the ketchup on page 131.

- -

CLASSIC KIMCHI WITH CHINESE CABBAGE AND RHUBARB

Makes about 700 g (1 lb 9 oz/4½ cups)

1 kg (2 lb 3 oz) Chinese cabbage
100 g (3½ oz) peeled mooli (daikon)
100 g (3½ oz) rhubarb
1¼ tbsp sea salt
150 g (5 oz/⅔ cup) Kimchi Base (see page 140)

Instructions:

1. Divide the Chinese cabbage lengthways, then cut it into 1 cm- (½ in-) thick slices. Use as much of it as possible, and do not be afraid to include the thick parts at the root.

2. Cut the mooli and rhubarb into thin matchsticks. Put the matchsticks into a bowl together with the Chinese cabbage and massage in the salt. Leave at room temperature for at least 1 hour so the fruit and vegetables have time to release their liquid. Stir and press the mixture from time to time.

3. Massage the kimchi base into the Chinese cabbage mix well. I usually wear rubber gloves when I'm doing this – it makes it easier to get to every nook and cranny, and you don't get red hands.

4. Sterilise a 1 litre- (34 fl oz-) jar (preferably one with a rubber sealing ring and metal clip such as a Kilner or Mason jar). Push the kimchi down into the jar a little at a time. Press on it with a wooden spoon so you get it all in (including the liquid). Close the lid and seal with the metal clip.

5. Put the jar on a plate, preferably with a plastic bag around it, as in all probability a fair bit of liquid will escape (just make sure you do not seal the bag at the top). Leave the jar at room temperature for 3–5 days. The longer it is left the more acidic it will be.

6. Put the jar in the fridge and leave for at least 1 week so the flavours have time to develop. The kimchi will form a spicy liquid, which can be used to flavour the ketchup on page 131.

Once, when I wanted to make kimchi and did not have enough time for it to mature properly, I had the idea of adding rhubarb to give an acidic boost. The result was twice as good as usual – the rhubarb contributed acidity, created a pleasant flavour dimension and gave it a Swedish twist. Since then I have always included rhubarb in my kimchi if it is in season.

SMOKED TOMATOES

Enough for 8-10 burgers

500 g (1 lb 2 oz) tomatoes
4 garlic cloves
2 sprigs fresh rosemary
4 springs fresh thyme
100 ml (3½ fl oz/scant ½ cup) olive oil
sea salt and freshly ground black pepper
smoking wood chips (see page 155)

Instructions:

1. Bring a large saucepan of lightly salted water to the boil. Fill a bowl with ice-cold water and place it nearby.

2. Cut a cross in the tops of the tomatoes. Blanch them by quickly immersing in the boiling water for 10–15 seconds until the skin starts to loosen. Take the tomatoes out with a slotted spoon and put them in the ice-cold water, then peel them and put them to one side to dry.

3. Take a large ovenproof dish and a smaller heat-resistant dish with a rim around 1.5 cm (½ in) high (the rim must not be higher than that of the large ovenproof dish). Put a thin layer of smoking wood chips at the bottom of the large ovenproof dish, then lay the smaller dish inside it. (If you cannot get hold of any smoking wood chips or do not have a barbecue at home you can simulate the smoky taste by sautéing the blanched tomatoes in a frying pan (skillet) with oil and a little liquid smoke.)

4. Light the barbecue.

5. Put the tomatoes, garlic and rosemary and thyme sprigs on the smaller dish and drizzle olive oil over them. Sprinkle with salt and pepper. Cover with foil and put the ovenproof dish together with the smaller dish in it on the barbecue while it is still actively flaming. After a few minutes the wood chips will start to smoke, and the smoke will wisp out under the foil (if the smoke does not appear, you can fold the foil up a bit at the corner to check it is smoking). Take the ovenproof dish off the barbecue when it starts to smoke and lay it on the ground for a few minutes. Repeat this stage three or four times. Remove the foil to check whether the tomatoes and the oil have developed any colour. If not, repeat the process a few more times.

6. Put the tomatoes into a sterilised jar, pour the oil over them and seal the jar. To bring out the flavours, you can fry the tomatoes quickly in a little oil just before serving.

The oil with the tomato juice is brilliant as a flavouring for a smoky Chipotle Mayonnaise (see page 126) - ideally together with a little saffron and vanilla.

21

ROASTED KALE

- -

Serves around 8-10 as a side

500 g (1 lb 2 oz) kale or cavolo nero
4 small garlic cloves
100 ml (3½ fl oz/scant ½ cup) olive oil
sea salt and freshly ground black pepper

Instructions:
1. Preheat the oven to 120°C (250°F/Gas ½).
2. Cut off the stem of the kale if it is thick and woody (this can vary from one sort to another, and depending on maturity, but as a rule I remove it).
3. Put the kale leaves and garlic on a baking tray and drizzle oil over them. Sprinkle with salt and pepper. Roast in the middle of the oven for 20 minutes.
4. Take the roasted leaves out of the oven and transfer to a wire rack with baking parchment underneath to catch any excess oil.

22

GRILLED AND STEAMED
SPRING ONIONS

Enough for 6 burgers

100 ml (3½ fl oz/scant ½ cup) olive oil
sea salt and freshly ground black pepper
6 spring onions (scallions)

Instructions:
1. Pour the oil into a ziplock bag big enough to accommodate the spring onions. Sprinkle with salt and pepper. Put the bag next to the barbecue so it is close at hand.
2. Light the barbecue. Lay the spring onions on the grid while the charcoal is still actively flaming. Cook the onions all over so the surface gets a little burnt.
3. Using tongs, transfer the spring onions to the ziplock bag. Seal the bag and shake it so the oil covers all the onions. Leave them in the bag for about 20 minutes so they steam in their own heat.

#23

DRY-ROASTED WALNUTS

Makes about 1 litre (34 fl oz/4 cups)

1 kg (2 lb 3 oz) walnuts with shells
  (500 g/1 lb 2 oz without shells)
2 tsp mild chilli powder, e.g. piment d'Espelette
sea salt

Instructions:
1. Crack open the walnuts and remove the shells.
2. Heat a dry frying pan (skillet), ideally a cast-iron one. Toast the nuts over a medium heat until they start to take on a little colour, for about 2 minutes. Shake the pan now and then so the nuts do not get too burnt, but don't worry if they burn slightly – it creates a good flavour.
3. Take the pan off the heat and season with chilli and salt.

#24

NUT BUTTER

Several of the burger recipes in this book include various types of nut butter – e.g. almond, cashew and hazelnut. You will find them in well-stocked shops, but be sure to only buy good-quality, natural versions – not the ones that have been sweetened with sugar. If you have a food processor with a knife blade at home it is extremely easy to make your own nut butter. Mix the nuts at maximum speed until you have a fine, smooth butter. This will take 10–20 minutes, depending on food processor, type of nut and quantity. Initially, a nut flour will form, but the nuts will gradually start to release oil, creating a buttery consistency. It is a good idea to have a spatula to hand so you can scrape the nut mass down off the edges. If it is still dry after 15–20 minutes you can pour in a little extra oil, such as peanut, coconut or rapeseed oil (do not use cold-pressed oil – the flavour of the oil must be as plain as possible).

handy to have in stock

Some of the ingredients in the book will not always
be available at your regular corner shop. Pop into
a well-stocked food shop or delicatessen and buy
the following vital ingredients so you have them
in your pantry the next time you feel like having
a green burger.

Peanut oil: An oil that withstands really high temperatures, and a clear favourite for deep-frying. The oil itself is fairly flavourless, which means it will not compete with the flavours of other raw ingredients. There is, however, a cold-pressed version with a really clear peanut flavour. If you find it, use it as you see fit, but I recommend that you only add it as seasoning, as you would do with a really good olive oil.

Nut butter: Cashew nut butter, almond butter, hazelnut butter, peanut butter – incredibly easy to make yourself, keeps for a long time in the fridge, and absolutely wicked for flavouring your burgers with. Buy it ready-made or make your own (see page 149).

Miso paste: The umami bomb! When I tried out miso paste as seasoning in the kimchi base instead of fish sauce it lifted the kimchi to a completely new level. Miso paste, in various forms, is sold in supermarkets as well as most Asian shops. I usually use an organic unpasteurised miso paste made of fermented grains and soy beans.

Vinegar: Malt vinegar, sherry vinegar and champagne vinegar are my favourites. I use malt vinegar for full-bodied dishes, and like putting sherry vinegar in Asian-influenced dishes (it reminds me a bit of sake, with its sweet, nutty note). For quick-pickling, e.g. of jalapeños, champagne vinegar is without peer.

Sichuan pepper: Available from well-stocked food shops, and has a flowery, citrusy, peppery flavour that is a bit chilli-like. Goes really well with coriander seeds and black pepper (see page 132) and I like using it for seasoning grilled or fried vegetables.

Panko breadcrumbs: Japanese breadcrumbs that create a crispiness that normal breadcrumbs get nowhere near. Unbeatable for deep-frying and for giving your patties a good consistency and texture. Used frequently and almost shamelessly in the recipes in this book.

Kelp: I use seaweed more and more often, to flavour stocks, when frying onions, grated over grilled vegetables, in marinades and sauces, and last but not least deep-fried, as in the recipe on page 93.

Mild chilli powder/piment d'Espelette: Chilli from the village of Espelette in the Nive valley in the French Basque Country. Personally I find that as a dried chilli seasoning it is unbeatable. It is big on flavour and has an ideal mild heat – unlike ordinary chilli powder, which often has a slightly acrid, strong chilli sting, but less flavour. Piment d'Espelette is available in many delicatessens, but you can also buy it online.

Smoking wood chips: Available in most shops selling barbecues and barbecue accessories. I use Abu smoking wood chips, which are normally used for smoking fish, but they work at least as well for smoking things such as tomatoes. As the wood chips are so fine they create smoke faster than other wood chips.

Black rice: Despite the name, this isn't rice but a type of grass. It looks good, is tasty and rich in antioxidants. Available from supermarkets.

Black garlic: Still a little tricky to get hold of, but we will doubtless be seeing more of it in the shops in future. Like miso paste it is a wonderful seasoning, and very different from ordinary garlic in its raw form. Mild and characterful, with a sweet toffee note, it has a consistency reminiscent of soft liquorice. You can also make black garlic yourself by wrapping garlic in cling film (plastic wrap) and leaving it in a food dehydrator set to 55°C (130°F) for three weeks.

Active charcoal powder: Sibylle's Bakery in Malmö, Sweden, sells a black loaf that I love, and this bread has formed the basis for the black charcoal buns in this book. The charcoal powder is above all for effect - the bread really does go jet black - but it also creates a lovely flavour, and Japanese tradition holds that it has purifying properties. I order my charcoal online through the Danish company Sort of Coal, which imports active charcoal made from charred pine needles from Japan.

First published by Bonnier Fakta, Stockholm, Sweden

Published in the English language by arrangement with
Bonnier Rights, Stockholm, Sweden

Published in 2017 by Hardie Grant Books, an imprint of
Hardie Grant Publishing

Hardie Grant Books (London)
5th & 6th Floors
52–54 Southwark Street
London SE1 1UN

Hardie Grant Books (Melbourne)
Building 1, 658 Church Street
Richmond, Victoria 3121

hardiegrantbooks.com

British Library Cataloguing-in-Publication Data. A
catalogue record for this book is available from the
British Library.

Green Burgers by Martin Nordin
ISBN: 978-1-78488-143-6

Editor: Hanna Jacobsson
Design: Katy Kimbell and Li Söderberg

For the English hardback edition:

Publisher: Kate Pollard
Senior Editor: Kajal Mistry
Desk Editor: Molly Ahuja
Publishing Assistant: Eila Purvis
Translation: William Sleath
Copy editing: Kay Delves
Typesetting: David Meikle

Colour Reproduction by p2d
Printed and bound in China by C&C Offset Printing

Thank you!

Nicola, for putting up with my experiments and always eating what I cook, even at 11:32 pm. For tolerating a photography studio in our kitchen for six months, with work surfaces crammed with spices, bags of flour, vegetables caked in soil, erupting jars of kimchi and the odd smoky experiment. And for believing in me and encouraging me to always do better.

Anton and Ellie, for also putting up with your dad manically running in and out of the kitchen and coming out with warnings such as: "You can't actually go into the kitchen right now, because your dad's going to deep-fry and use a blowtorch and take bread out of the oven, all at the same time." And for giving the thumbs-up for roasted kale, sweet-potato bread and homemade ketchup.

My mother, father, sister and brother, for also being supportive and showing love and understanding – especially my brother, for constantly editing the text and checking my photos.

My foodie friends: Alex, for keeping my interest in food at a high level. Victoria, for always wanting to talk food and for pushing me and getting me to believe in what I'm doing. Anna, for your pep talk and your commitment to food in Malmö. Henrik, for all the chat and for great advice on bread. Ann-Katrin Braf, for your inspiring ceramics, which frame my food and make it more attractive.

Malmö's restaurants, because right now you are offering the most exciting food in Sweden. Many recipes in the book are inspired by food I have eaten locally, especially at eateries such as Bastard, with Andy at the helm, and Saltimporten Canteen, with Sebbe and Ola. Thank you for creating such an incredibly congenial food climate in Malmö.

Gourmetboulevarden on Östra Rönneholmsvägen in Malmö, OST & Vänner, for introducing Belper Knolle, which I can no longer live without, Petra at Ola & Ko with her pickles, eggs and piment d'Espelette, and not least Sibylle's Bakery, for their inspiration around charcoal bread.

Johan at Bokeslundsgården, for your commitment and for being a one-off with an absolutely incredible drive in terms of getting the best results from your lovely farm in the best possible way.

Oskar, for helping me believe in my snaps, for taking such crazily cool photos and for taking pictures of me for this book – pictures I actually like.

My new-found friends at Bonnier Fakta. Eva, for finding me, believing in me and pushing me in the right direction, Hanna, for your positive involvement and for supporting me as I crossed the finishing line, and especially for endorsing most of the recipes by trying them out yourself. And Li and Katy, for your fabulous illustrations and design.

Huge thanks!